KEATS, POE, AND
THE SHAPING OF CORTÁZAR'S MYTHOPOESIS

PURDUE UNIVERSITY MONOGRAPHS
IN ROMANCE LANGUAGES

William M. Whitby, General Editor
Allan H. Pasco, Editor for French
Enrique Caracciolo-Trejo, Editor for Spanish

Associate Editors

I. French

II. Spanish

Volume 8

Ana Hernández del Castillo

Keats, Poe, and
the Shaping of Cortázar's Mythopoesis

ANA HERNÁNDEZ DEL CASTILLO

KEATS, POE, AND

THE SHAPING OF CORTÁZAR'S MYTHOPOESIS

AMSTERDAM / JOHN BENJAMINS B. V.

1981

Contents

Abbreviations . . . . *vi*

Acknowledgments . . . . *vii*

Foreword . . . . *ix*

Introduction 1

Part 1: The Magna Mater

   1. Woman as Circe the Magician 17
   2. Woman as Death 43

Part II: Rites and Mysteries

   3. The Individual Quest 71
   4. The Collective Quest 93

Conclusions 109

Notes 115

Bibliography 127

Abbreviations

The following abbreviations have been used to refer to Cortázar's works:

E	— *El examen,* unpublished MS, written at Buenos Aires, 1948-50, kept by Cortázar in Paris. Used by permission.
IJK	— *Imagen de John Keats,* unpublished MS, written at Buenos Aires-Paris, 1948-52, kept by Cortázar in Paris. Used by permission.
LR	— *Los reyes* (Buenos Aires: Angel Gulab, 1949).
B	— *Bestiario* (Buenos Aires: Sudamericana, 1951).
OP	— Edgar Allan Poe, *Obras en prosa,* trans. and prologue by Julio Cortázar. (Madrid: Revista de Occidente, 1954).
F	— *Final del juego,* 2nd ed. (Buenos Aires: Sudamericana, 1964; first ed. México, 1956).
AS	— *Las armas secretas* (Buenos Aires: Sudamericana, 1958).
P	— *Los premios* (Buenos Aires: Sudamericana, 1960).
R	— *Rayuela* (Buenos Aires: Sudamericana, 1963).
VDOM	— *La vuelta al día en ochenta mundos* (México: Siglo XXI, 1967).
62	— *62: Modelo para armar* (Buenos Aires: Sudamericana, 1968).
UR	— *Ultimo round* (México: Siglo XXI, 1969).
PM	— *Pameos y meopas* (Barcelona: Ocnos, 1971).
PO	— *Prosa del observatorio* (Buenos Aires: Sudamericana, 1972).
LM	— *Libro de Manuel* (Buenos Aires: Sudamericana, 1973).
O	— *Octaedro* (Buenos Aires: Sudamericana, 1974).
FCVM	— *Fantomas contra los vampiros multinacionales* (México: PEPA, 1975).

Cortázar's quotes of Keats's letters refer to *Letters of John Keats,* ed. Maurice Buxton Forman (London: Oxford University Press, 1948). I have used Hyder E. Rollins, *The Letters of John Keats: 1814-1821,* 2 vols. (Cambridge, Mass.: Harvard University Press, 1958).

All references to Poe's works, unless otherwise specified, pertain to *The Complete Works of Edgar Allan Poe,* ed. James A. Harrison, Virginia ed., 17 vols. (New York: T. Y. Crowell, 1902).

All references to Keats's works pertain to *Poetical Works,* ed. Heathcote William Garrod (Oxford: Clarendon Press, 1958).

Acknowledgments

I owe the greatest debt to Julio Cortázar, who provided encouragement and friendship, answered numerous questions, and allowed me to scrutinize the unpublished manuscripts for *El examen* and *Imagen de John Keats*. Anna Balakian and Aileen Ward of New York University and Ana María Barrenechea of Columbia University provided guidance and criticism during the early stages of this study. I wish to thank Djelal Kadir and Roberto González-Echevarría of PUMRL for their careful reading of my typescript and their valuable suggestions. My friend Mari-lynn Jiménez of Mount Holyoke College read an earlier version and offered welcome advice and help. Carlos, Ana, Paula, and Fred lent me their unwavering affection and support.

Foreword

The formative role which the works of John Keats and Edgar Allan Poe play in the works of Julio Cortázar, including the elaboration of Cortázar's poetics, is well attested to both by Cortázar's own readings and preferences and by the widespread influence of these two writers upon generations of European and Latin American writers who also influenced Cortázar. Both the direct and indirect influence of Keats and Poe upon Cortázar can be carefully traced.[1] Cortázar's own admissions, his early readings and writings, and the unmistakable affinity of his theories to those of his two predecessors offer substantial proof of this dual influence. A more important and general question is raised, however, by the fact that Keats and Poe seem to be the dominant influence in Cortázar's work: Which aspects of the works of the two Romantics have been kept and transformed by Cortázar's imagination? Is there a common bond in the works of Keats and Poe which is also the common denominator for the works of Keats, Poe, and Cortázar? And finally, why these particular images, themes, or ideas? Thus, we are concerned here with identifying not only the specific images and themes that Cortázar may have borrowed from Keats and Poe but also what in the nature of these images and themes made them adaptable to Cortázar's own imagination. Obviously, an individual writer, regardless of how heavily he is influenced by a predecessor, does not reproduce an exact copy of the latter's work. The individual writer, like an entire culture or age, takes from the past only what it can bring to life or use in the present, what is, to use a much maligned as well as misused term, *relevant* to its own needs and problems. The past, according to T. S. Eliot, exists to be reshaped by the present into its own image. Similarly, Cortázar reshapes certain themes and images he found in Keats and Poe which struck a sympathetic chord in his imagination in *his own* medium, a modern idiom for the modern writer.

The images that Cortázar reshapes into a modern idiom are those which are archetypal in character; that is, if we analyze the images and themes which Cortázar borrows from his predecessors we shall find that most of them are not the idiosyncratic ones, the ones that belong concretely to the experience of Poe and Keats as individuals, but the ones which represent variations of well-established archetypes. Thus, at this point, we cease being concerned with just the direct influence of Keats and Poe upon Cortázar to become involved with the concept of archetypes; for, at the most profound and vital level of the imagination, at least in this case, the effect of influence, which is historical and factual, becomes the operation of atemporal archetypes and myths, the patterns of experience common to man as a whole. However, the concept of personal influence does not disappear, for what Cortázar inherits from Keats and Poe is not merely a schematic pattern which may be found in many texts both primitive and modern but a pattern which had been modulated in a specific way. The archetypal descent into a nether world, for example, may be found throughout the mythologies of the world; but for the Romantics, and especially Poe, this descent into a nether world was carried out through the heedless plunge into the world of the irrational and of extreme emotions. The underworld of the gods of death and destruction of primitive thought becomes the habitat of the irrational, the abnormal, the excesses of the sensual within man himself. The way to reach this world is through Rimbaud's famous "dérèglement de tous les sens," through drugs, through the experience of man's least controllable emotions—passion and fear. The structure of the quest remains the same—the descent into a nether world; the content of the chthonic, however, changes its nature. Cortázar translates this pattern, which has been given a different content not only by the Romantics but by the European culture of the eighteenth and nineteenth centuries as a whole, into a modern idiom by intellectualizing the "dérèglement des sens" of Rimbaud. The "descent" of Horacio Oliveira, for example, is no longer impelled by the irrational forces which drove Arthur Gordon Pym to the limits of the world, but by a deliberate, intellectual experimentation with the irrational and the abnormal as a means to some other world, to some other knowledge. The contemporary hero does not plunge into the chthonic world with the same élan as Rimbaud in "Le Bateau ivre." Whereas the Romantic hero indulged himself in extreme sensations innocently, that is, without being self-conscious, because he was the first to do it, the contemporary hero cannot escape from the self-consciousness which is characteristic of modern thought. The contemporary hero, from Broch's Virgil to Sartre's Roquentin, is a man who is constantly rethinking the experiences which he has had, and Horacio Oliveira is no exception. When Horacio comes into contact with the nether world, in the chapter with the *clocharde*, for example, his intellect is absorbing and integrating that "raw" experience into an intellectual system and tradition. No Romantic hero would have stopped to consider Heraclitus' experiment in the midst of such an experience.

Thus, we may legitimately speak of influences through archetypes. The Romantics employed and modified a well-known quest pattern; this "romanticized" pattern is then taken up in various forms by contemporary writers, such as Cortázar. The process is analogous to that of the life of an organism. An organism inherits certain immutable patterns which define its species; however, the individual organism itself presents a unique configuration, which conforms to the pattern of the species but is an individual variation thereof. Archetypes are the original pattern; literary tradition may be seen as modifications of this pattern; and finally the creativity of the individual writer brings the archetype to life in a unique form. It is important, therefore, to establish the links between Poe, Keats, and Cortázar in order to know the specific, modified archetype which Cortázar reshapes. An analysis of this complex relationship must be carried out simultaneously at the level of archetypes and the level of influence; to deny or suppress one aspect in favor of the other is to simplify the reality of the poetic process implied in the concept of "chameleonism." To write from a poet's world rather than about it, one must absorb the very substance of that world; and archetypal images form the substructure, the underpinnings of that substance. The interpenetration of both aspects, the archetypal and the personal influence, must then be constantly kept in mind when evaluating the unique manner in which Cortázar combines and incorporates various elements from Keats's and Poe's works into his own.

Introduction

> . . . *ninguno de los grandes contemporáneos de John—Wordsworth, Coleridge,*
> *Byron, Shelley—agrupa en su poesía (siempre mayor en cantidad y tiempo*
> *que la de Keats)* tantos temas brotados del subsuelo ancestral, *de la tierra*
> *incógnita y común que continúa dándonos todos los años, en todos los*
> *lugares de la tierra, esas flores verbales idénticas e inmutables que son caperu-*
> *cita, barba azul, piel de asno, cupido y psiquis, ondina, circe, pulgarcito.* . . .
> *Ya nadie ignora que esos relatos son supervivencias de una mecánica ritual,*
> *restos enormemente alterados de conductas primitivas, ae tabúes y compor-*
> *tamientos; que no hay diferencia entre la mano que traza los bisontes en*
> *Altamira y la que en nuestra infancia temerosa confiaba las llaves del palacio*
> *a la tonta esposa que pronto abriría la estancia vedada.* . . .

Julio Cortázar
Imagen de John Keats

Throughout his theoretical essays, Cortázar has singled out the unique quality that, for him, distinguishes the true artist from the mere craftsman. This quality—somewhat similar to Keats's "negative capability"[1]—resides in an essential passivity on the part of the artist and an attuning of his psyche with the "primitive forms," or rather, "primordial forms," that seek expression through him.[2]

This basic idea in "Para una poética" is reaffirmed in "Del cuento breve y sus alrededores," where the author distinguishes between those stories that are merely the result of literary skills and the far superior ones that result from what he terms a "possession" by forms that arise from "an undefinable and ominous territory" (*UR*, pp. 37-38; my translation).

For Cortázar, the great short story "installs itself inside the reader"—just as it does inside the writer—and fascinates him, lifting him from a faded, monotonous reality, and hurling him into an intense, numinous realm (*UR*, p. 38). This concept of a creative rapture or "possession" plays a prominent role in Cortázar's fiction, as well, from the very beginning. The preparation of Delia's poisons ("Circe," *B*), Alina Reyes' verbal games ("Lejana," *B*), the meticulous ritualistic care of the "mancuspias" and the rabbits ("Cefalea" and "Carta a una señorita en París," respectively, *B*), the children's games in "Los venenos" and "Final del juego" (*F*), down to Oliveira's rescue of the fallen sugar-plum (*R*), Andrés Fava's "initiatic voyage" to the chateau of Verrières (*LM*), and the journeys in "Manuscrito hallado en un bolsillo" (*O*), all offer ample evidence of an interest in the ritualistic that constitutes, in fact, one of Cortázar's constant and distinctive traits. The pecularity of Cortázar's ritualistic structures—as evinced in the stories mentioned above—lies in their relationship to unusual or abnormal mental states.

In his analysis of the creative process in "Del cuento breve y sus alrededores" (*UR*), Cortázar discusses his own "raptures" ("Lo que sigue se basa parcialmente en experiencias personales cuya descripción mostrará, quizá . . . algunas de las constantes que gravitan en un cuento de este tipo," *UR*, p. 36). Then, he likens these experiences to Poe's:

> El hombre que escribió ese cuento pasó por una experiencia todavía más extenuante, porque *de su capacidad de trasvasar la obsesión dependía el regreso a condiciones más tolerables.* . . . Esto permite sostener que cierta gama de cuentos *nace de un estado de trance*, anormal para los cánones de la normalidad al uso, y que el autor los escribe mientras está en lo que los franceses llaman un "état second.". . . Que Poe haya logrado sus mejores relatos en ese estado (paradójicamente, reservaba la frialdad racional para la poesía, por lo menos en la intención) lo prueba más acá de toda evidencia testimonial el efecto traumático, contagioso y para algunos diabólico de "The Tell-Tale Heart" o "Berenice.". . . Si Poe hubiera tenido ocasión de hablar de eso, estas páginas no serían intentadas, pero él calló ese círculo de su infierno y se limitó a convertirlo en "The Black Cat" o "Ligeia.". . . (*UR*, pp. 38-40; my italics)

By offering an explanation that would elucidate both Poe's creative process and his own, Cortázar reasserts his earlier identification with Poe as writer in "Del sentimiento de no estar del todo," from *La vuelta al día*. His explanation, moreover, follows the directives of the Jungian theory of inspiration to which Cortázar had originally referred in *Imagen de John Keats*, as we shall see.

Jung's theory describes archetypes as the guiding forces in the process of *transformation* or spiritual development:

> The impact of an archetype, whether it takes the form of immediate experience or is expressed through the spoken word, stirs us because it summons up a voice that is stronger than our own. Whoever speaks in primordial images speaks with a thousand voices; he enthrals and overpowers, while at the same time he lifts the idea he is seeking to express out of the occasional and transitory into the realm of the ever-enduring. *He transmutes our personal destiny into the destiny of mankind*, and evokes in us all those beneficent forces that ever and anon have enabled humanity to find refuge from every peril and to outlive the longest night. . . . *The creative process.* . . . *consists in the unconscious activation of an archetypal image, and in elaborating and shaping this image into the finished work.* By giving it shape, the artist translates it into the language of the present, *and so makes it possible for us to find our way back to the deepest springs of life.* [My italics][3]

When Cortázar justifies the success of a number of his short stories by saying that they "escape oblivion because I have been able to receive and transmit without great losses those *palpitations of a deep psyche*, and the rest comes from a certain ability not to falsify the mystery, to keep it *as near as possible to its source, with its original tremor, its archetypal uttering*" (*UR*, p. 42; my italics and translation), he identifies his theory of the creative act with Jung's.

Apparently, around 1950—as he was halfway through his book on Keats—Cortázar became acquainted with the theories of depth psychology, especially through Daniel Devoto's well-updated library which, as we read in the manuscript itself, became one of his most important sources of information in matters of mythology and anthropology. Halfway through his study—specifically upon undertaking his analysis of *Lamia*—Cortázar embarks on a long digression about matriarchal archetypes and rites of passage, expressing his amazement at what he sees as the considerable recurrence of these in Keats's works. Henceforth, he regularly resorts to concepts of depth psychology in order to explain Keats's poems.

In this respect, Cortázar's interest in the psychological aspects of myth and ritual reflects a tendency of Argentine letters during the thirties and forties; as Jorge B. Rivera indicates, the decade of the forties crystallized a number of contributions to the theory of myth introduced by the periodical *Sur* since 1931. During these years, the magazine popularized a number of recently published works which helped to define the theory of the *archetypal*. These works were, principally, Frazer's *The Golden Bough*, Levy Brühl's studies about the primitive mentality, Jung's theories about the archetypes and the collective unconscious, and D. H. Lawrence's discussions on the panic irrationality of vital forces.[4] In spite of their heterogeneity, these works have one trait in common: they all deal with myth and ritual as symptomatic of mental processes and revelatory of the structure of the psyche.

The outlook expressed through these works influenced a whole generation of Argentine writers; as Graciela de Sola demonstrates in her study of Argentine letters during the forties and fifties,[5] a deep religiousness and a tendency towards mysticism emerge as the common denominator of the works produced in Argentina during these years. Such characteristics are particularly prominent in the works of three of Cortázar's closest friends at this time: Eduardo Jonquières, Daniel Devoto, and Alberto Girri. Daniel Devoto's work, especially, was deeply influenced by Jung's theories; it was in Devoto's library that Cortázar found the treatises that shaped the outlook on myth he displays in the second part of *Imagen de John Keats*. On the other hand, the works of Leopoldo Marechal[6] had been influenced by René Guénon's studies on mythology and religious science in general.[7] Ernesto B. Rodríguez and Osvaldo Svanascini, similarly, reflect the interest in myth and ritual so characteristic of these years.[8]

In *Otras inquisiciones*, Borges had amply referred to the term "archetype" in its Platonic and Schopenhauerian sense. Borges had used the word "archetype" to refer to eternal concepts (Ideas) that reappear in different ages under similar guises. Borges had pointed out the Romantic poets' special grasp of these "archetypes" in his essays "La flor de Coleridge," "El sueño de Coleridge," and "El ruiseñor de Keats," and he specifically referred to Jung by name in "Nathaniel Hawthorne."[9] Even if his tone betrays a certain ironic condescension (he remarks that Jung's theories are gathered in "beautiful, homogeneous volumes"), the mention itself shows that he was very much aware of the currency of Jung's theories.

From his early study "La urna griega en la poesía de John Keats," Cortázar had stressed Keats's ability to recapture the psychic reality behind ancient myths and render them alive in his poems. Later, in *IJK*, upon undertaking his analysis of *Lamia*, Cortázar makes a number of crucial statements that reveal his own poetic sensitivity to myth while he discusses Keats's. He refers to the mythic themes in Keats's works as *"temas brotados del subsuelo ancestral"* (*IJK*, p. 266; his italics). He sees the structures in Keats's works as "supervivencias de una mecánica ritual, restos enormemente alterados de conductas primitivas" (*IJK*, p. 267) which persist because a dark instinct within us makes us create them anew with each generation, obeying the obscure commands of the collective unconscious. Keats, he proceeds, not only preserved the intuition of the child but was also capable of apprehending the *psychic contents* (Cortázar's italics) of infancy. Keats was "possessed" by these themes, which were charged with "ancestral truths" and denoted "la sobrevivencia inarticulada del hombre primitivo." Even Keats's lack of a "formal" education favored his instinctive approach to myth, Cortázar continues (*IJK*, p. 267). He defines Keats's method, then, as "una rabdomancia poética"; unconsciously, in "negative capable moods" he chose themes pregnant with magic and hidden suggestions. Cortázar proceeds to provide a kind of "statistics" in order to show the archetypal themes and characters he perceives in Keats's works (*IJK*, pp. 269-70). Finally, he concludes that the impulse which guided Keats in his choice of themes "subyace en la región donde la poesía es *charme*, incantación, sortilegio: el lugar donde el mago vencido cede su vara al poeta que continuará en otro plano su tarea de dominación" (*IJK*, p. 270).

This study bears an enormous relevance to Cortázar's formative process as a writer; his analysis of the use of myth in Keats's works acted as a major force in shaping the poetic theory Cortázar outlined in his article "Para una poética," which otherwise displays so many points of contact with other aspects of the book on Keats, as I have shown elsewhere.[10] It was through his discussion of Keats, primarily, that Cortázar defined his concept of the poet as one who is "possessed" by the magnetic forces of the collective unconscious and thus manifests, in his writings, "archetypal" themes and figures. The importance of Keats's influence in the development of Cortázar's concept of inspiration is confirmed when we consider that Cortázar, who, having been a professor of nineteenth-century English literature at the University of Cuyo, was acquainted with the writings of Wordsworth, Coleridge, and Shelley, singled out Keats as *the one* English Romantic who was most responsive to the promptings of the collective unconscious:

> Invito solamente a esta verificación: ninguno de los grandes contemporáneos de John—Wordsworth, Coleridge, Byron, Shelley—agrupa en su poesía (siempre mayor en cantidad y tiempo que la de Keats) tantos *temas brotados del subsuelo ancestral*, de la tierra incógnita y común que continúa dándonos todos los años, en todos los lugares de la tierra, esas flores verbales idénticas e inmutables. (*IJK*, p. 270; his italics)

The recurrence, in later articles, of the basic ideas and terminology put forth by Cortázar in *IJK* further evinces his absorption and complete internalization of the concepts first employed in connection with Keats. "Del cuento breve y sus alrededores," written nearly twenty years after *IJK*, is a good case in point. In it, Cortázar restates the poetic theory previously expressed in "Para una poética," an article that had derived from an analysis of Keats's poetics:

> Pero si el acto poético me parece una suerte de magia de segundo grado, tentativa de posesión ontológica y no ya física como en la magia propiamente dicha, el cuento no tiene intenciones esenciales, no indaga ni trasmite un conocimiento o un "mensaje." El génesis del cuento y del poema es sin embargo el mismo, nace de un repentino extrañamiento, de un desplazarse que altera el régimen "normal" de la conciencia. (*UR*, p. 42)

The expressed connection between Cortázar's use of Jungian terminology and his application of it to the works of Keats and Poe poses a methodological problem: How can we study the relationship between these works in terms of direct "influence" when the themes and structures in question are seen as manifestations of the collective *unconscious*? On the other hand, how can we use the word "unconscious" to refer to parallel figures and structures between Cortázar's works and those of Keats and Poe when we know that Cortázar spent a number of years studying the works of these authors and even singled out the very themes and structures that he considered had been dictated to these writers by the collective unconscious, and later reproduced them in his own works? Moreover, how can we even speak of an "unconscious" appearance of archetypes in the works of a writer who had been acquainted with Jung's theories from the early years of his career, used Jungian terms to express his own poetics, and was, thus, aware of the archetypal forms arising from the collective unconscious? Evidently, the case in question calls for a combined approach where *both* the concept of archetypes and that of direct influence must be recurred to. For, if it is true that an unconscious process might be called to account for Cortázar's choice of these authors and his singling out of those themes and figures in Keats's and Poe's works that appealed to his own sensitivity and that of his times, it is also true that the direct contact with these two authors—the only ones to whose works he dedicated a full-length study or a complete translation, respectively—left a definite imprint on the way in which Cortázar perceived, shaped, and presented a number of archetypal figures and structures.

In the following chapters, I will consider the extent to which Cortázar's studies of Keats and Poe influenced his own presentation of the archetype of the Magna Mater and of the quest structures. The relevance of the archetype of the Magna Mater for Cortázar is pointed out by the author himself, who, in the previously discussed section of *IJK*, evinced an uncommon fascination with what he saw as the survival of matriarchal rites in Keats's works. The evidence of the impact this aspect of Keats made on Cortázar is to be found in the latter's treatment of the Feminine immediately after his study of Keats and thereafter throughout his career. Cortázar, who was abandoned by his father at the crucial age of five and was raised by his mother and spinster aunts in a Buenos Aires suburb, felt, as he has himself implied,[11] a profound uneasiness regarding women, which was reflected in the nonhuman or mythical representation of the Feminine in his works, as we shall see. His contact with Keats's works resulted in the confirmation and strengthening of Cortázar's tendency for dealing on a subliminal plane with a subject too dreaded to be confronted directly. The mythic projection of the Feminine in Keats's works exerted a magnetic attraction on Cortázar, who found, in this process, a way to exteriorize his inner fears through the poetic representation of Woman under the many faces of the Magna Mater.

A more complex situation is presented when dealing with Cortázar's response to Poe's use of myth. Firstly, Poe had been affected, particularly by way of Charles Anthon, by the new and revolutionary theories about myth that had swept through New England roughly between 1820 and 1860.[12] These theories had placed a considerable emphasis on the symbolic value of ritualistic actions characteristic of myth. Although Cortázar never actually discussed the archetypal themes or characters presented in Poe's stories themselves or the unconventional character of his use of myth, there is a greater *textual* evidence of Poe's influence than there is of Keats's in Cortázar's works. If Keats's influence can be sensed behind the *conception* of the Feminine's archetypal projections, Poe's can be confirmed in actual textual parallels. What happened is, apparently, that Cortázar's study of archetypes and archetypal structures in the works of Keats ended by influencing his own perception of these in the works of Poe, who had remained as an unconscious, completely internalized model for Cortázar's works throughout his career. So, just as his earlier article "Para una poética" had started as a study of Keats's chameleonism and ended very close to a definition of Poe's vampirism,[13] so now his study of archetypes in the works of Keats ends by absorbing not only Keats's but also Poe's archetypal characters and structures, particularly the theme of descent into the nether world, which had provided the basic symbolism for "MS. Found in a Bottle," "A Descent Into the Maelström," and *The Narrative of Arthur Gordon Pym.*

I have found no information with which to date the exact time when Cortázar first became acquainted with Jung's theories; judging, however, from references in his articles and from the book on Keats itself, I have assumed—as previously stated—that his encounter with Jung took place around 1950, through Borges' lectures and Devoto's library. Now, there is no evidence in the passage about matriarchal archetypes to show that Cortázar possessed a *thorough* knowledge of Jung's theories; aside from the use of terms such as "collective unconscious," "constellations," "profound psyche" and his account of the process through which Keats—according to him—conceived the poems centering on the matriarchal archetype, most of his references are to Andrew Lang and Saintyves, who—while pioneers in new approaches to myth, anthropology, and folklore—had little to do with Jung's theories. Yet Cortázar's own works, and particularly the way in which he absorbed and transformed certain figures and themes from Keats and Poe, indicate, as we shall see, a later and more thorough acquaintance with the Jungian studies on the relationship of dream symbolism and mythological symbolism to the structure of the psyche. From my own conversations with the author, I know he was acquainted not only with the works of Jung himself but also with Joseph Campbell's *The Hero With a Thousand Faces* (first published in 1948)—a work which he highly recommended—and Erich Neumann's *Art and the Creative Unconscious* (first published in 1959), which contains an essay on "Leonardo da Vinci and the Mother Archetype." I do not know exactly *when* he read these books, and I have found no mention of them in his essays. These studies apparently provided additional information on themes he had first chosen instinctively. A different role was destined for Keats's works, particularly *Lamia* and "La Belle Dame sans Merci," which were directly connected with Cortázar's study of archetypes in Keats's works. Keats was the first poet Cortázar studied in terms of the Jungian theory of inspiration—or even *saw* in terms of this theory, from the evidence provided by his essays—and Keats's *Lamia* and "La Belle Dame" continued to haunt the conception of his feminine characters throughout his career. Later, the concept was applied to Edgar Allan Poe, and the ghost of Ligeia and *Pym*'s White Avenger appeared, from then on, behind the climactic scenes in his novels.

Before discussing Cortázar's absorption and transformation of feminine archetypes in the works of Keats and Poe, I shall attempt to define the aspects and implications of the Magna Mater archetype according to the principles of depth psychology. In my discussion I shall rely, basically, on the theories put forth by Erich Neumann in *The Great Mother*,[14] the most complete analysis of the archetype to date. I must state, however, that the categories here established will be used only as a frame of reference; in order to facilitate the discussion of the particular aspects of the archetype Cortázar perceived in each author and later developed; I do not intend to imply that Cortázar was consciously studying Keats and Poe under the light of Neumann's theories. Nor do I claim that either Keats or Poe, in a rare feat of rhabdomantic inspiration, anticipated Neumann and Jung by one century. In any case, a concept of the Magna Mater very similar to Jung's had appeared as early as 1815 in George Stanley Faber's *On the Origin of Pagan Idolatry*. Moreover, Johann Jakob Bachofen's *Das Mutterrecht* (first published in 1856) and Robert Briffault's *The Mothers* (published in 1927) had discussed the archtype years before Jung or Neumann; as Neumann states, representation precedes explanation. Great Goddesses appeared in mythology and art centuries before the term "Magna Mater" arose; Keats and Poe did not need to *know* about a concept of the Magna Mater to conceive their extremely complex feminine characters. But Cortázar's acquaintance with such a concept helped refine his sensitivity towards and perception of the Feminine in the works of Keats and Poe.

When Cortázar uses the words "matriarchal" and "matriarchal rites," he is utilizing the word in its Jungian sense; that is, he means more than just "maternal." In analytic or depth psychology the term "matriarchal" is generally applied to that which contains and absorbs, whether human or inanimate. The Great Mother is, thus, the fundamental, basic archetype, since it deals with man's first experiences: being contained in the womb and being expelled at the moment of birth. Likewise, it is later associated with man's last experience: being received in the womb of the Earth Mother after death. As Neumann observes, " 'Mother' in this connection does not refer merely to a relationship of filiation but also to a complex psychic situation of the ego, and similarly the term 'Great' expresses the symbolic character of superiority that the archetypal figure possesses in comparison with everything human and with created nature in general" (*GM*, p. 11). Thus, the Great Mother is associated with whatever the ego perceives as supernatural, awesome, and threatening. One of the archetype's essential characteristics is that it combines both positive and negative attributes. Just as primitive man, whose consciousness was not yet differentiated and capable of establishing categories, experienced a paradoxical simultaneity of good and evil, friendly and terrible, in the figure of a primordial goddess that encompasses both aspects, so does a modern man, fixated at an early stage of consciousness through psychological trauma, become overwhelmed by the psychic contents of the Mother archetype and imaginatively represent it in forms similar to those that have appeared in mythology through the ages. Neumann synthesizes the idea discussed above observing that "the archetype of the Magna Mater is a mythological motif and that, as an 'eternally present' content of the collective—i.e., universal human—

unconscious, it can appear equally well in the theology of Egypt or the Hellenistic mysteries of Mithras, in the Christian symbolism of the Middle Ages or the visions of a modern psychotic" (*GM*, p. 15). For modern man, the archetype appears as a compensation for an overemphasis on consciousness; it acts as a means for dealing with unconscious contents too horrible to face directly, and it contains both conscious and unconscious elements. The term "constellation"—to which I will refer in the following chapters—is related to the rise of archetypes. A "constellation" is the symbolic relationship established by the conscious mind between a current problem and the dormant archetypes in the unconscious; through the "constellation," the otherwise "neuter" archetype becomes activated and acquires a specific form (i.e., the anima archetype is "constellated" as Circe, Lamia, or Diana) which becomes revelatory of the individual's psychic configuration.[15]

The schemata provided below will simplify the understanding of the elements comprising the archetype and of the forms through which it manifests itself.

Schema I presents six levels in the formation and representation of the archetype; of these, I shall omit discussion of levels one, two, and three, since they refer to primitive states of consciousness that have no relevance to this study. Level four is pertinent to us for, even though it refers to a relatively elementary form of consciousness that does not apply to any of the three authors in question, it presents the basic manifestation of the Magna Mater archetype. She has three forms: the good, the terrible, and the good-bad mother. Good Mother, Terrible Mother, and Great Mother form a cohesive archetypal group. Level five is directly related to this study since it deals with the ego's perception of the archetype as it appears in dreams, in visions, or in the imagination. At this level, the archetype appears basically as "anima," or as the agent that sets in motion the process of *transformation*. Level six presents a further stage of complexity; it deals with the world as the outward plane of projection on which the projected inner images are experienced through figures or persons. Since this level deals with the externalization of inner fears, it also encompasses the manifestations of Magna Mater figures in literature and art. Here we find the projection of mythological figures on persons or on literary characters. The figure of the Gorgon, the sight of whom turns men into stone, is a projection of the Terrible Mother, while Sophia, as divine wisdom, is a projection of the Good Mother. The figure of Isis, combining characteristics of the two, corresponds to the archetype of the Great Mother. A modern artist can project the figure of the Gorgon onto a woman who transfixes a man with terror, such as Hélène in *62*, or the figure of Isis onto a woman who acts as an agent of inspiration but who is also capable of "tearing apart" the man's consciousness, thus becoming the object of dread, such as la Maga in *Rayuela*.

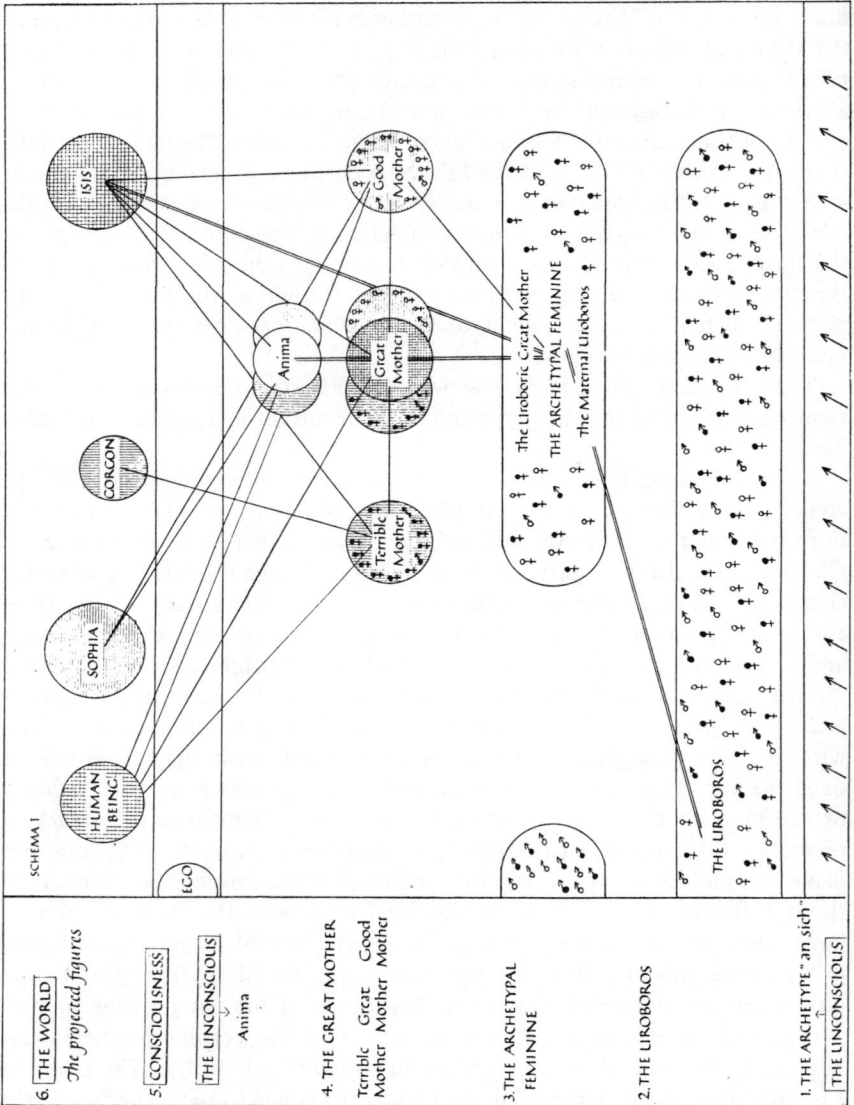

SCHEMA I—Rise and Differentiation of the Mother Archetype. Erich Neumann, *The Great Mother: An Analysis of the Archetype*, trans. Ralph Manheim, Bollingen Series XLVII, p. 19. Copyright 1955 by Princeton University Press. Reproduced by permission.

My second schema—Neumann's Schema III—deals with the symbolic projections of the Feminine and their division into four basic categories: the
elementary character (M, for "mother"), positive and negative, and the transformative character (A, for "anima"), positive and negative. The elementary
or maternal aspect appears when consciousness is relatively undeveloped and
the individual is childlike and dependent on unconscious forces or impulses.
It also refers to a concern only with the satisfaction of physical necessities
and with corporeal fulfillment in general. Keats's "idyllic bower" in *Endymion*,
with its dependence on a feminine figure (Venus) as the provider of pleasure
and fulfillment, would be an example of this category. The transformative
character is not antithetical to the elementary, but derives from it and is intimately connected with it. Its emphasis, however, falls on amplification
and change, rather than on the preservation of what exists. The anima is
the manifestation *par excellence* of the transformative character, since, by
captivating man, she sets him in motion and impels him toward change. The
two aspects of the Feminine, while intimately connected, are yet distinct.
While the elementary character (the Magna Mater) tends to dissolve consciousness, the transformative character (the anima) fascinates, but does not oblit-
erate; it inspires change and transformation. Even though the process of
transformation itself offers perils to the soul or consciousness, it leads to
destruction of the ego only when the Great Mother is preponderant over the
anima. Neumann observes that these mixed situations are characteristic of
certain creative men, particularly among the Romantics, some of whom were
"wholly dominated by this constellation in which the mother archetype of
the collective unconscious overpowers the anima and by its fascination leads
to the uroboric incest of the death urge or to madness" (*GM*, p. 34). Madness
and death urge in these writers, and particularly in Poe and Cortázar, is interpreted as the desire to extinguish consciousness and melt into the body of the
Mother/Death, as we shall see.

The two perpendicular axes in Schema II—Neumann's Schema III—correspond to the two characters of the Feminine previously discussed: M stands
for the elementary character (accent on the maternal); A stands for the transformative character (emphasis on movement and change). Both axes have an
upper, positive pole (the Good Mother, the anima as Sophia, the Virgin Mary)
and a lower, negative one (the Terrible Mother, the anima as Circe, the
Gorgon). The circles in the schema deal with the different manifestations of
the archetype in the various stages of consciousness and related to various
psychic processes. I shall not be concerned with the circle at the center, which
represents the earliest stage of consciousness, dominated by the elementary
character and its functions of bearing and releasing or holding fast and fixating.
Nor shall I be concerned with the second circle (which deals with the transformative character of the female), but rather with the third circle, or the

F+

MOTHER VIRGIN

MARY MARY

SOPHIA

DEMETER

M+ Good Mother A+ Positive Transformative Character

immortality Spiritual wisdom Inspiration Mysteries

Vegetation Mysteries rebirth Transformation vision

ISIS birth inspiration MUSE

fruit ecstasy

development Transformation transformation sublimation

bearing Elementary Character giving
releasing

Containing

rejection holding fast
deprivation fixating
ensnaring

sickness

transformation diminution extinction
dissolution devouring

Mysteries of Drunkenness ecstasy death Death Mysteries KALI

LILITH madness
CIRCE dismemberment M- Terrible Mother

A- Negative impotence
Transformative stupor
Character

HECATE

ASTARTE GORGON

YOUNG WITCH F- OLD WITCH

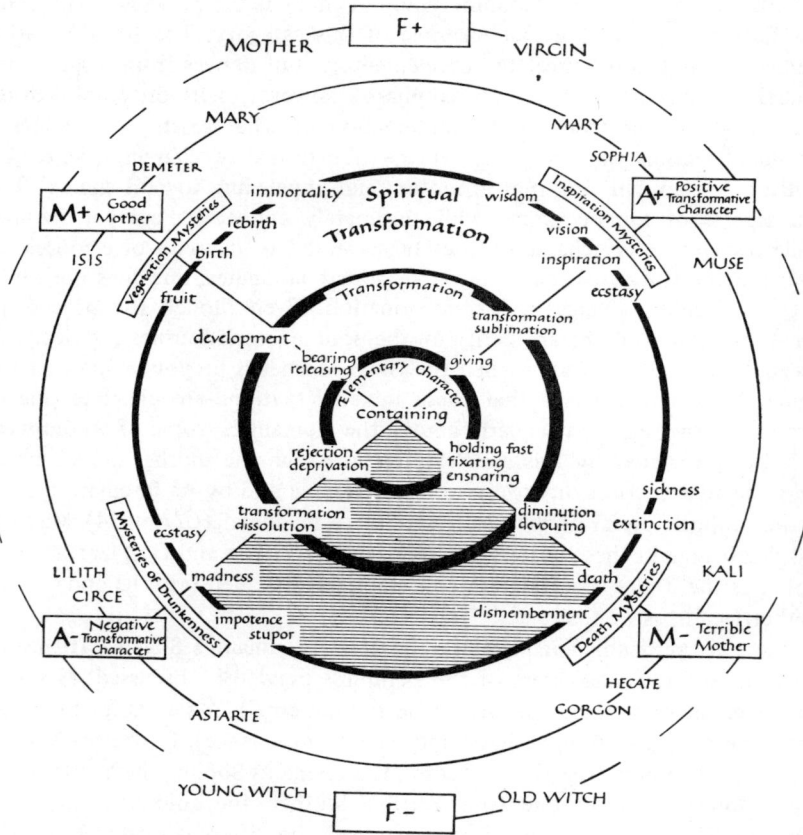

SCHEMA II—Manifestations of the Mother Archetype. Erich Neumann, *The Great Mother: An Analysis of the Archetype,* trans. Ralph Manheim, Bollingen Series XLVII, p. 82. Copyright 1955 by Princeton University Press. Reproduced by permission.

realm of spiritual transformation, and the symoblic figures of goddesses associated with it. The four intersections of the axes with the circle of spiritual
transformation correspond to four categories of feminine mysteries, or rituals,
meaning not only the concrete enactment of mystery festivals but the psychic
sphere of unconsciously related symbols. To the *death mysteries* (M−) belong
the rites of goddesses of death and the dead, as well as symbols having to do
with the burial of the dead and all sacrifices leading to death. Death, extinction,
rending to pieces are the core of the negative pole M, which primarily deals
with *sacrifice* and ritual execution. Pain and sickness, as conditions that
weaken and kill, also belong in this context. In this relation, I shall discuss
a number of symbols of diminution, rending, annihilation, rot and decay (for
their association with graves and cemeteries), and negative death magic. Here
the Mother appears as Kali, the devouring goddess of death. To this pole
belongs the symbolism of Poe's maelstrom, sea, caves, and putrefaction,
particularly as they appear in *Pym*, as well as the symbolism in Cortázar's
El examen, Los premios, and parts of *Rayuela.*

To the negative pole M belong all goddesses representing the Terrible
Mother: Kali of India, Gorgon of the pre-Hellenic age, Hecate, terrible Ishtar,
Isis, Artemis of Asia Minor, the goddesses of the Underworld and the dead
in general. Also included are negative demonic figures such as the Furies, lamias,
empusae, and so on. These goddesses belong to the most primitive stage of
human consciousness prior to the phase when they appear as goddesses; often,
when superseded by the domestic gods, they regress to a preconfigurative stage
(*GM*, p. 80). They appear, then, as the cave, the labyrinth, the ship, or as
absorbing waters; such is the case in Poe's maritime tales and in the previously
mentioned works by Cortázar.

The axis M+ refers to the *vegetation mysteries*, indicating development
and growth. Here, we are concerned with the fertility rituals to the Great
Mother, which have to do with growth and the increase of life. These do not
play a significant role in the authors we are dealing with, or at least in
Cortázar's perception of them. To axis A+, *inspiration mysteries*, belong all
phenomena dealing with the spiritual-psychic realms of manticism and magic.
These culminate in the creative climax of vision and inspiration, and all that
brings about the positive development of the personality and consciousness.
This is the locus of the divine virgins and the Muses, and also of Athene and
Artemis. Cortázar's la Maga, throughout the first half of *Rayuela*, belongs to
this axis. We also find here more complex figures of goddesses, like Artemis,
who, as Great Goddess of Asia Minor, also includes attributes of poles M+
and M−.

The negative pole A refers to the *mysteries of drunknness*, which, initially
related to vision and inspiration, end by bringing about the dissolution of
consciousness. Pole A− pertains more to a spiritual-psychic death than to a
physical death, as in the death mysteries of the Terrible Mother or "old witch."

The negative intoxicant, poison, and all that leads to stupor, enchantment, helplessness, and dissolution belong to the sphere of seduction by the "young witch." Also, this pole deals with negative orgiastic sexuality, leading to the extinction of consciousness and to madness; in this case, ecstasy is produced, but it reduces and disintegrates the personality instead of broadening it. Rejection and deprivation are the characteristics of the negative anima, whose best manifestation is the Belle Dame sans Merci and whose symbols are the archetypal attributes of forsakenness and nakedness, exposure and banishment into the void.

Cortázar—more inclined to symbolic representations of situations that deeply disturbed him than to their discussion and analysis—found in Keats's mythic projection of the Feminine a gate leading to the poetic confrontation with a number of issues he could not face directly. Thus what we find in his works is not a spontaneous rise of archetypes, but rather a semi-conscious channeling of impulses long present in himself through the study of the feminine archetypes in Keats's works.

Still, Cortázar continued—parallel with the new development of the mythic projection of the Feminine—to represent woman through nonhuman symbols, that is, through objects and precincts and even animals that allude to the Terrible Mother's ferocious, devouring, absorbing, or annihilating qualities. This had been—from the beginning—a trait he had shared with Poe; but if we compare the symbolism of his first novel, *El examen*, with that of the second, *Los premios*, we realize the degree to which this characteristic became intensified with the development of Cortázar's style. Two main events are to be associated with this development: first, the book on Keats, which refined Cortázar's perception of the symbolism of the Feminine; and second, his translation of the complete prose works of Poe from 1953 to 1954. In studying the central symbolism of the Feminine—whether as mere primitivistic symbolism or in a more elaborate mythic representation—I shall be discussing a number of symbols which Neumann presents as being properly identified with the Terrible Mother: the tomb, the devouring maw, the engulfing waters, and to a certain extent, the ship and the labyrinth (*GM*, pp. 45-48). After establishing— with the help of Neumann's concepts—the degree to which Keats's and Poe's archetypal manifestations of the Feminine are reflected in Cortázar, I shall proceed to evaluate the extent of such an influence in the presentation of the rites or mysteries through which the hero is meant to come to terms with the Feminine principle as represented by the Magna Mater.

PART I

The Magna Mater

1

Woman as Circe the Magician

The mother has from the outset a decidedly symbolical significance for a man, which probably accounts for his strong tendency to idealize her. Idealization is a hidden apotropaism; one idealizes whenever there is a secret fear to be exorcized. What is feared is the unconscious and its magical influence.

C. G. Jung
"Psychological Aspects of the Mother Archetype," *Symbols of Transformation*

The universal goddess makes her appearance to men under a multitude of guises; for the effects of creation are multitudinous, complex, and of mutually contradictory kind when experienced from the viewpoint of the created world. The mother of life is at the same time the mother of death; she is masked in the ugly demonesses of famine and disease.

Joseph Campbell
The Hero With a Thousand Faces

In his book on Keats, Cortázar repeatedly expresses his admiration for Keats's capacity to respond to "the promptings of the collective unconscious." From the ensuing discussions, however, it becomes clear that Cortázar is mainly concerned with Keats's response to one archetype in particular: the archetype of the Great Mother, particularly in her aspect of Terrible Mother. In Cortázar's view, Keats becomes the first of the Romantics to rediscover the powerful symbolism of Mother Goddesses, whose worship dates back to the dawn of man's consciousness. In one of the most impassioned passages of his book on Keats, Cortázar proceeds to present a "statistics" showing the recurrence of matriarchal figures and matriarchal rites in Keats's poetry,[1] emphasizing the uniqueness of Keats's poetry in the richness of its archetypal contents. He underplays, thus, the equally important role of Coleridge's "Christabel" or of the figure of Death in "The Rime of the Ancient Mariner" (Coleridge had conceived these poems in analogous trancelike states that could have been interpreted, likewise, as "seizures by the archetypes of the collective unconscious").

Cortázar's appreciation of the important role played by goddess figures in Keats's poetry, on the other hand, is not groundless or far-fetched; Walter Evert has stressed Keats's special sensitivity to the figure of the moon goddess, observing that "lunar references and encomia are abundant in his pre-Endymion poetry, and that—as one might expect from a person of Keats's sensitivity—he was moved not only by the variousness of the moon's appearances but also by the appearances of other objects touched with its light."[2] He proceeds to observe that not only in *Endymion* but also in "I Stood Tip-Toe" and others of Keats's early poems the moon receives the paean otherwise reserved for Apollo; it is she who inspires the poet, she who is associated with the principle of "light": "She has for all practical purposes become identical with him."[3] If Apollo is associated with the light of day, and thus, of intellectual pursuits, Cynthia, as ruler of the night, guides the poet into a more obscure, intuitive, and magical knowledge. Similarly, Robert Graves, in *The White Goddess*, had seen Keats as a "goddess-poet," that is, as one who is especially receptive and responsive to the numinous projections of the Feminine.[4] As his major biographers—especially Aileen Ward and Robert Gittings[5]—observe, there is an important link between Keats's difficulty in establishing relationships with "real" women and his portrayal of the goddesses around whom his major poems are built. It has been perceptively observed that there was in Keats's mind—more than in any other of the Romantic poets—a strong compulsion towards the realization of physical love which conflicted with his idealization of woman as goddess: consequently, Keats's erotic scenes either flee too far away into mythology or fall into segments of bad taste. Physical love can never be portrayed actually and directly, but must be clothed in Renaissance garb ("Isabella"), medieval lore ("The Eve of Saint Agnes"), or Greek myth (*Lamia*); a situation involving an actual woman will be bound to create a dramatic crisis.[6] Indeed, women always perplexed Keats; his attitude towards them shows a mixture of contempt for the superficiality of the "blue-stockings" and dread for the magical powers of the "Charmians."

In a letter to Bailey (22 July 1818) Keats had explored the reasons behind his feeling of uneasiness when dealing with women, attributing it to the disappointment he felt upon finding out that real women fell "so beneath my Boyish imagination. . . . When I was a Schoolboy I though[t] a fair Woman a pure Goddess, my mind was a soft nest in which some one of them slept, though she knew it not."[7] He reveres the ideal concept of women that he carries in his mind and feels somewhat guilty at the thought that he expects too much from the real women he meets. Moreover, he longs for the feminine presence, yet he feels extremely awkward in the company of most ordinary women he meets. Further in the same letter, he tells Bailey: "I must absolutely get over this—but how? The only way is to find the root of evil, and so cure it 'with backward mutters of dissevering Power.' That is a difficult thing; for an obstinate Prejudice can seldom be produced but from a Gordian complication of feelings, which must take time to unravell(ed) and care to keep unravelled."[8] Cortázar is right, then, when he perceives the complexity of Keats's relationship to women and establishes a connection between his "Gordian complication of feelings" regarding real women and the peculiar conception of his feminine characters. His interpretation takes a definite turn away from conventional Keatsian criticism, however, when he concentrates exclusively on the *negative* aspects of the Feminine presented in Keats's letters and works, disregarding all others.

Cortázar's study singles out the figure of Circe (*Endymion*, III) as the basic "constellation" of the Feminine in Keats's early works and as the nucleus from which the figures of "La Belle Dame sans Merci" and *Lamia* later derived. Cortázar then establishes a connection between the basic constellation of woman as "Circe the Magician" and the conflicts that characterized Keats's relationships to women. Next, Cortázar presents Keats's affair with Fanny Brawne as the poet's desperate struggle for self-preservation facing the deadly, absorbing, annihilating enemy: Woman.

Again, Cortázar's interpretation is not wholly groundless; and Keats's early critics had, in fact, literally blamed Fanny Brawne for Keats's death.[9] Before meeting Fanny Brawne, Keats apparently tended to divide women into two groups: those who were sexually attractive (the "Charmians") and those who were "good" (like Georgiana, his brother George's wife).[10] When he met Fanny he was confronting, for the first time, a woman who was both. The tragedy of Keats's passion for Fanny Brawne and its effect upon the poet's physical and mental health has been the subject of endless controversy among Keats's critics, who are often at variance in their interpretation of how "fatal" Fanny really was for Keats. It is indeed a difficult matter to deal with; for if we take Keats's last letters as the main evidence of the conflict—as Cortázar appears to have done—the presence of Fanny appears to have been, indeed, lethal. Keats's letters to Fanny Brawne describe a kind of feeling that goes far beyond the "normal" passion of man for woman and closely approaches the devotion of a would-be saint about to be martyred for his religion. In a letter of 13 October 1819 we read:

> I cannot exist without you—I am forgetful of everything but seeing you again—my Life seems to stop here—I see no further. You have absorb'd me. I have a sensation at the present moment as though I was dissolving—I should be exquisitely miserable without the hope of soon seeing you. . . . I have been astonished that Men could die Martyrs for religion—I have shudder'd at it—I shudder no more—I could be martyr'd for my Religion—Love is my religion—I could die for that. I could die for you. My Creed is Love and you are its only tenet. You have ravish'd me away by a Power I cannot resist; and yet I could resist until I saw you; and even since I have seen you I have endeavoured often "to reason against the reasons of my Love." I

> can do that no more—the pain would be too great. My love is selfish—I cannot breathe without you. (Forman, Letter 16)[11]

Keats is "seized" by Fanny's presence, seen as "a Power I cannot resist" and as one he cannot explain away by means of reason. It is a passion that threatens with the dissolution of the self, and yet it is a state that, once known, cannot allow the poet to fall comfortably back into his former existence. He must pursue the state of ecstasy even at the cost of his own destruction. The expression "exquisitely miserable" illustrates, through the power of the opposition of feelings in it, the central nature of his experience. It is analogous to the "pleasurable pain" of the odes and of *Lamia*; it is a feeling that combines the extreme of joy with the extreme of pain, attaining a conjunction of opposites that blend as one in the instant where the self is about to dissolve.

Most of Keats's critics agree in drawing a relationship between the poet's meeting of Fanny Brawne and his conception of certain poems centering on the identification of love and death and on the appearance, in other poems, of the figure of the sorceress that provides both the acme of sensuous pleasures and the destruction of the unwary man who succumbs to her charms. The poem "Bright Star"—conceived soon after Keats met Fanny Brawne—expresses a theme destined to become almost obsessive for the later Keats: the identification of the moment of accession to the ideal with the moment of death. Only in the image of a climactic death can Keats resolve the opposing emotions aroused by Fanny: the longing to attain the most intense joy of possession, and the dread of dissolution and loss of the self in that very intensity. The erotic metaphor "to melt into" reappears in "The Eve of St. Agnes" to refer to the consummation of Madeline and Porphyro's love. The idea that the star is a poetic transposition of Woman in general and Fanny in particular seems confirmed by Keats's letter to Fanny of 25 July 1819, where he calls her "fair star."[12] But the identification between love and death, merely suggested up to this point, finds a definite expression in the haunting poem "La Belle Dame sans Merci," also written soon after Keats met Fanny Brawne. In both "La Belle Dame" and the later and longer *Lamia*, a sorceress charms an unwary dreamer, luring him away from his path and sequestering him in an "elfin grot" or an enchanted palace, away from human pursuits, and occasioning his death upon the withdrawal of her love. Both poems display the same central idea, intimately related to the feeling in the previously quoted letter from Keats to Fanny: once the heights of pleasure derived from the possession of the ideal have been tasted, a return to ordinary pursuits becomes impossible. The sorceress disappears, but her memory remains to drive her victims insane and drain the life away from them. Thus there were enough facts in Keats's letters and late poems to lay the foundations for a theory where Woman would appear as Keats's arch-enemy, and Cortázar's own experiences made him intensify this aspect of the poet's relationship with women.

Cortázar was already thirty-five, and still unmarried, when he wrote the book on Keats. According to his own declarations to Luis Harss, he was a confirmed bachelor at the time, led a secluded life, and had few friends.[13] He had lived with his mother until he was almost thirty; as previously noted, he was abandoned by his father when he was five years old and was raised by his mother and aunts in the Buenos Aires suburb of Bánfield. If—according to Cortázar—the constellation of the Feminine as Circe, magician and seductress, had been the predominant image in Keats's unconscious, the figure of Parsifal's mother seems to have arisen as the basic constellation in his own unconscious. Both in conversation and in a letter,[14] the author spoke of his identification as a youth with the hero of the Grail legend; and Austin, the youthful hero of 62, is also likened to this hero (62, pp. 89, 172, 209). If the constellation of the feminine archetype serves to determine—according to analytical psychology—the nature of a man's future relationships with women, the images of Circe and Parsifal's mother will help us to define the basic difference between Keats's and Cortázar's conflicts with the Feminine.

Most of the artists best admired by Cortázar resemble him in one central, extremely important point—they were fatherless. Keats and Poe, the objects of this study, were no exceptions. However, unlike Keats, Poe—and Saki, Baudelaire, Edward Lear, René Magritte, Ambrose Bierce, and other writers with whom Cortázar liked to identify—led lives marked by incidents and relationships which were analogous to incidents and relationships in Cortázar's life, thus favoring his identification with them. Identification at the level of artistic aims was not sufficient for Cortázar; he needed to feel a more personal bond with these authors, as well, in order not only to achieve a "chameleonic" passage into their poetic selves but also to find a confirmation and reassurance of his own existence through theirs: Saki, Magritte, and Lear were also raised by spinster aunts; Baudelaire and Bierce were uncommonly and even abnormally attached to their mothers; all were pestered by asthmas, allergies, and other psychosomatic ailments associated with mother-fixation. Yet, if Poe, Baudelaire, Bierce, and Saki displayed sensitivities and aesthetic aims that were akin to Cortázar's, Keats did not. As I hope to have shown elsewhere,[15] Keats's sensitivity is so different from Cortázar's that Keats's influence appears only in the form of certain images or in general outlines of concepts that Cortázar completely reworked and transformed, even though he still referred to these as "Keats's principles." The difference between both authors' sensitivities is dramatically manifested in the contrasting constellations of the Feminine in each. Circe is basically the *sensuous* enchantress, the "young witch" whose ambivalence as gate to both positive inspiration and negative intoxication is partly linked to the hero's own attitude towards her. As previously discussed, Circe is the archetypal manifestation of the negative anima and, as such, subject to defeat by a hero capable of outwitting her or taming her *through the body*. Parsifal's mother is basically a *spiritual* figure; as mother—

rather than anima—she inspires a greater awe and, as such, a far greater danger. Parsifal's mother—who held fast to her son, dressing him in women's clothes to prevent him from joining the knights (as her husband, Parsifal's father, had done) and from leaving her side—has the symbolic power to emasculate and nullify; she is the spiderlike, possessive, devouring Terrible Mother.[16] If Keats's early poems show woman, primarily, as the young, sensuous enchantress and the provider of pleasure, Cortázar's stories symbolically show woman as a disembodied, absorbing *presence* analogous to Poe's maelstrom, seas, and—most important—houses ("Casa tomada," "Cefalea," "Relato con un fondo de agua"), and his later tales present the towering, spiderlike Mother of "Cartas de mamá," "La salud de los enfermos," and "El otro cielo."

In spite of this basic difference in the perception of the Feminine, Cortázar seems to have compensated by emphasizing other points of contact between himself and Keats that would favor a "chameleonic" incursion into the latter's world: both were inclined to prefer the "ideal" over the "real," both came from modest backgrounds in literary milieus dominated by the upper classes, both possessed a certain unsophisticated naiveté in their early careers which often made them the objects of scorn.[17] A biographical detail provided yet another: Cortázar fell in love with Aurora Bernárdez—who became his wife in 1952—at the time when he wrote *IJK*. Through his comments on Keats, he manifested feelings which were surprisingly akin to those Keats himself had recorded on the margins of Burton's *Anatomy of Melancholy* at the time when he first felt attracted to Fanny Brawne. Cortázar's comments on Keats, like Keats's on Burton, display a violent misogynism, an intensely felt conflict between love and freedom, and a desire to reject woman for the sake of poetry.[18]

Cortázar, exercising the chameleonism of his poetic theory, attempted to place himself within Keats's self in order to absorb the vision of the Feminine that had so fascinated him. In the chapter on Fanny Brawne, Cortázar speaks, almost in the first person, from Keats's world; yet, the Keats he presents us is a new Keats, fashioned after Cortázar's own heart. For Cortázar, Keats's *affective* conflict appears as a *mental* problem; his anxiety facing women, as an insurmountable dread and a *desire to reject*. Earlier in his book, Cortázar had observed that in the sudden appearance of Miss Jane Cox, Keats had seen "al enemigo, al usurpador" who pretended to monopolize his attention and take him away from poetry. Keats's letter, however, states: "I always find myself more at ease with such a woman. . . . I am at such times too much occupied in admiring to be awkward or on a tremble. I forget myself entirely because I live in her."[19] But Cortázar, after describing the profound impression Miss Cox had made on Keats, states that "con la misma violencia del deseo surge el rechazo" (*IJK*, p. 169). Violent rejection? What Keats actually says is "I don't cry to take the moon home with me in my Pocket not [for "nor"] do I fret to leave her behind me."[20] Yet Cortázar claims that Keats "se alza violento contra la sospecha de que la mujer sea ese símbolo engañoso de la pluralidad en la unidad, el abregé del mundo para comodidad de poetas" (*IJK*, p. 169). What happens is, apparently, that Cortázar interpreted the reference further in Keats's letter to George and Georgiana ("Since I wrote thus far I have met with that same Lady again, whom I saw at Hastings and whom I met when we were going to the English Opera") as an allusion to Miss Cox (Charmian), and thus, he attributes Keats's repudiation of marriage in the same letter as a "violent rejection" of Miss Cox. The "lady of Hastings," however, was not Charmian, but Isabella Jones; Cortázar's mistake regarding the lady's identity is understandable enough, since "the lady of Hastings" was not identified as Mrs. Jones until 1952,[21] this is, the same year Cortázar finished his book on Keats.

However, even if we were not to suspect—as we now do—that Keats's "violent rejection" of Mrs. Jones apparently ended in the poet's affair with that lady,[22] we would still find Cortázar's interpretation of Keats's tirade about women somewhat exaggerated. Here is the passage in question:

> Notwithstanding your Happiness and your recommendation I hope I shall never marry. Though the most beautiful Creature were waiting for me at the end of a Journey or a Walk; though the carpet were made of Silk, the Curtains of the morning Clouds; the chairs and Sofa stuffed with Cygnet's down; the food Manna, the Wine beyond Claret, the Window opening on Winander mere, I should not feel—or rather, my Happiness would not be so fine, a[nd] my Solitude is sublime. Then instead of what I have described, there is a Sublimity to welcome me home—The roaring of the wind is my wife and the Stars through the window pane are my Children. The mighty abstract idea I have of Beauty in all things stifles the more divided and minute domestic happiness—an amiable wife and fine Children I contemplate as part of that Bea[u]ty—but I must have a thousand of those beautiful particles to fill up my heart. I feel more and more every day, as my imagination strengthens, that I do not live in this world alone but in a thousand worlds. . . . These things combined with the opinion I have of the generallity of women—who appear to me as children to whom I would rather give a Sugar Plum than my time, form a barrier against Matrimony which I rejoice in.[23]

In it, most of Keats's invectives—which are mild enough—are actually directed *against the institution of marriage*, not against women themselves, as Cortázar implies. Even the final remark about women achieves an identification between them and children—it does not liken women to Gorgons or spiders, as Cortázar's interpretation seems to suggest.[24]

Neither in his comments about Keats's meeting with Miss Cox nor in the chapter about Fanny Brawne (Isabella Jones he completely disregards) does Cortázar refer to Keats's struggle to overcome his anxieties regarding women; in Cortázar's interpretation, Keats is as blasé as Baudelaire about his misogynism. Nor does he ever allude to the positive aspects of Keats's relationship with Fanny Brawne. He observes that Keats's love for Fanny was not a passion *but a destruction*; thus, he literally interprets the bereaved and terminally ill Keats's accusations to Fanny as the poet's final statement in the affair. But he totally disregards that side of Keats's love through which the poet sought a fulfillment of his whole self. Cortázar overlooks the brighter side of Keats's love for Fanny (expressed in passages from his letters such as the following: "I never knew before what such a love as you have made me feel, was; I did not believe in it; my Fancy was afraid of it, lest it should burn me up. But if you will fully love me, though there may be some fire, 'twill not be more than we can bear when moistened and bedewed with Pleasures . . .").[25] Cortázar declares that Keats retreats in horror when faced with the possibility of love: "Su gusto por las mujeres que ofrecen una misma sensualidad se ve de pronto helado ante la sospecha del encarcelamiento. ¿Y el resto del mundo? ¿Y la libertad, la poesía, *el dolce far niente*, la llave de la calle?" (*IJK*, p. 302).

A greater injustice is to be found in Cortázar's portrayal of Fanny Brawne. He presents Fanny as a vampire who will attempt—even unawares—to suck the life out of a helpless, enthralled Keats. He observes that Fanny will not be motivated to destroy Keats by any particular cruelty of her own, but by her very feminine nature: *because she is a woman*. The desire to possess, absorb, and destroy the male is, for Cortázar, the very essence of the feminine nature. And so he observes:

> El cometa Brawne entraña, más que una pasión, *una destrucción*, y no es del todo casual que la primera crisis reveladora de la enfermedad de John cerrara el año inaugural de su amor, que tan amargamente lo había hecho feliz. Sin culpa de Fanny; nada que reprocharle, pobre muchacha. En todo lo que sigue deberá entenderse que no le pido peras al olmo, y que es John quien, desesperadamente, busca ser leal a sí mismo en contra de Fanny, *busca que Fanny sea otra, sea lo que una mujer no puede ser*. (*IJK*, p. 302; my italics)

Identifying with what he sees as Keats's perception of the "evil" side of women, Cortázar discusses the poet's approach to the Feminine through mythological allusions. He embarks on a consideration of what he sees as the recurrence of matriarchal archetypes in Keats's works in an attempt to understand, absorb, and incorporate his procedures. But his discussion of archetypal figures in Keats's works follows the pattern previously established in his discussion of the role of women in Keats's life: he stresses only the *negative* aspects of the matriarchal archetype manifested in Keats's works, disregarding all others. His study focuses on those mythological figures that will later reappear as the feminine protagonists of his own novels and stories.

In Cortázar's discussion of what he sees as the martriarchal archetypes presented in Keats's works, he rightly observes that the episode of Circe's bower in Book II of *Endymion* contains the seeds of both "La Belle Dame sans Merci" and *Lamia*. Likewise, in his discussion of "La Belle Dame," he expresses the opinion that this poem contains "la horrible revelación de que la dulce y llorosa doncella que el caballero encontró a la vera del camino y llevó es Circe la eterna, es la dominación y la degradación del amante bajo los filtros de la Maga" (*IJK*, p. 219). In effect, while Book II of *Endymion* had presented the bower of Venus and Adonis as the acme of sensuous love (where a perennially childlike Adonis depended on the generous Good Mother figure of Vénus [axis M+ in my Schema II]), Book III does present the contrasting bower of Glaucus and Circe, where the lover is degraded under the spell of the sorceress, as Cortázar points out. Glaucus falls in love with the nymph, Scylla, who rejects him. Seized with despair, Glaucus calls Circe to his aid. She, however, offers him her own love instead, trapping him in a net of love-dreams he cannot break away from:

> Who could resist? Who in this universe?
> She did so breathe ambrosia; so immerse
> My fine existence in a golden clime.
> She took me like a child of suckling time,
> And cradled me in roses. Thus condemn'd,
> The current of my former life was stemm'd,
> And to this arbitrary queen of sense
> I bow'd a tranced vassal . . .
>
> (III, ll. 453-60)

Circe acts first as a source of inspiration—in the role of anima—provoking a state of sensuous "ecstasy" in Glaucus; however, as Cortázar stated, she soon causes the reversal of this condition by turning the ecstasy into horror when she reveals her true face, mocking Glaucus' weakness and submission to her:

> Ha! ha! Sir Dainty! there must be a nurse
> Made of rose leaves and thistledown, express
> To cradle thee my sweet, and lull thee: yes,
> I am too flinty-hard for thy nice touch:
> My tenderest squeeze is but a giant's clutch.
> So, fairy-thing, it shall have lullabies
> Unheard of yet: and it shall still its cries
> Upon some breast more lily-feminine.
>
> (III, ll. 570-77)

The "reversal" or sudden overturning of ecstasy into its opposite is typical of situations where the "negative" anima is involved. As Neumann observes, sensuous ecstasy, or the ecstasy derived from drugs, alcohol, and other stimulants, is initially positive, since these substances set the unconscious in motion and may lead to transformation. Their effect easily becomes reversed, however, if the ego is overcome and "lost" in the intensity of ecstasy; if the will becomes totally extinguished, the originally positive experience leads to stupor, madness, impotence, or loss of self. The episode of Circe—which so fascinated Cortázar, so sensitive to the contradictory character of the Feminine—exemplifies the danger of loss of self implied in the abandonment to orgiastic sexuality. Glaucus, unable to keep a hold on himself, regresses to the position of the child regarding the mother, to the stage of the suckling who depends on the mother for the satisfaction of his needs. The stories in *Bestiario* were written roughly at the same time as the book on Keats; there appears to be a connection, then, between Cortázar's comments about Keats's Circe and the conception of the story he wrote under the same title. Cortázar's early story "Circe" (*Bestiario*) already displays this author's fascination with the figure of the mythical enchantress. There is a basic difference, however, between Cortázar's treatment of the sorceress and Keats's; Cortázar's Circe already displays the overlapping of the characteristics of the A— and M— sides of the archetype, as previously established. Basically, the negative anima is not a deadly figure. She is not "terrible" in the same sense as the Magna Mater; even when she seeks to destroy the male's consciousness, a positive reversal is possible, for she is always subject to defeat. As Neumann observes, "when Circe, the enchantress who turns men into beasts, meets the superior figure of Odysseus, she does not kill herself like the Sphinx, whose riddle Oedipus has solved, but invites him to share her bed" (*GM*, p. 35). Keats's Circe turns Glaucus into "an animal," but does not kill him; Cortázar's Circe, on the other hand, *is* deadly, displaying characteristics of the Terrible Mother, as well as the negative anima.

   In Delia Mañara, the mysterious girl who kills her suitors, we find a re-creation of the myth of Circe the Magician, the Lady of the Animals who absorbs the will of men, especially younger men (Delia is 22, Mario 19), and forces them into submission. Cortázar had praised Keats for his ability to re-create the *essence* of myths; his story accomplishes precisely this. Whether in ancient Greece or twentieth-century Buenos Aires, the situation is one and the same: a young boy, Mario, is enthralled by a mysterious woman who symbolically castrates him. The description of Delia—lithe and snakelike—is meant, from the very beginning, to corroborate the identification with the mythical sorceress implied in the title: Delia "era fina y rubia, demasiado lenta en sus movimientos" (*B*, p. 92); "A veces la escuchaba reirse para adentro, un poco malvadamente y sin darle esperanzas" (*B*, p. 93). Later in the story we are told that "Todos los animales se mostraban siempre sometidos a Delia, no se sabía si era cariño o dominación" (*B*, p. 94). Moreover, the reaction of Mario is in strict accordance to the myth: he breaks all ties with family and friends and becomes completely absorbed by Delia. The means she employs to ensnare and trap her victims—magical liquors and potions she stuffs into candies and feeds to her suitors—are also in harmony with the dynamics of the archetype. Medicines as well as poisons are agents of *transformation* and manifest that process in themselves (the sequence from plant to juice, juice to elixir, etc.).[26] But there is a more "terrible" aspect in Delia that is not usually characteristic of the archetypal Circe. Circe provides her victims with the positive ecstasy of sensuality before she turns them into animals. Not so Delia, who is totally destructive and absorbing. Her own last name, Mañara, is phonetically associated with "maraña" (web) and "araña" (spider), aside from being identical with that of Don Miguel de Mañara, Valle-Inclán's diabolical Marqués de Bradomín, whose female counterpart she appears to be. The deaths of the two suitors are also in agreement with the dynamics of the archetype; the first dies of a heart attack, an accident associated with the Terrible Mother's function of "fixating" and "paralyzing," and the second becomes bereaved and drowns himself, exemplifying her power to "drown" consciousness and "absorb" the personality.

Mario, however, escapes from Circe's clutches by *seeing* and *understanding* the symbolic action she performs as a prelude to her destruction of him. He sees the family cat dying in a corner of the kitchen, its eyes perforated with wooden splinters.[27] Then he presses the chocolate Delia hands him and discovers that the attractive chocolate exterior hides a filling made of cockroaches. She pierces the cat's eyes in the same way that she intends to destroy Mario's vision, that is, his consciousness. The eye, the site of consciousness, is one of the most important weapons of the hero in his battle against the Magna Mater, whose realm is that of darkness and "blind" instinct. On the other hand, the chocolate is symbolic of Delia herself; the repulsive, parasitic insect in her hides under an attractive exterior. Mario is able to escape from Delia's clutches by understanding or "seeing" her true nature. She is returned, at the end of the story, to the character of the "defeatable" negative anima.

From the above discussion, it becomes evident that there is no actual resemblance between Keats's and Cortázar's Circe, aside from the name itself and the ambiguous feelings towards women the authors displayed through them. The influence of Keats in this instance, then, must be traced to the mere conception of the feminine figure in mythological terms, but not to the actual representation. A similar situation is presented in "El ídolo de las Cícladas" and "Las ménades," both inspired by the sacrifices in honor of the ancient Mother Goddesses. I do not know whether Cortázar's interest in sacrifices originated in connection with his study of Keats or if it anteceded it; his own statement in *IJK* suggests that there was a simultaneous interest in both and that he somehow made a connection between the two, with or without grounds. In his commentary on the ode "On a Grecian Urn" (a reworking of his 1946 article "La urna griega en la poesía de Keats"), Cortázar exhibits—perhaps more blatantly than in any other section of his book—a tendency to attribute to Keats his own reactions to certain themes. He interprets the scene portrayed on the Grecian urn as a scene of *sacrifice*, with maenads dancing around the victim; he states that Keats's susceptibility to themes connected with matriarchal rites had made him conceive of such a scene. What this comment actually reveals is *Cortázar's* propensity to perceive the Feminine under the guise of Terrible Mother. The author's interest in ritual at the time when he wrote the book on Keats is responsible for the conception of "El ídolo de las Cícladas" and "Las ménades."

In "El ídolo de las Cícladas," Cortázar's choice of the Cycladic islands for the setting of the story is not accidental; Asia Minor is the site where the worship of a Terrible Goddess first arose. Neumann observes that these pre-Mycenean idols—dating back to 3000 B.C.—show a tendency towards abstraction that is not present in other primordial fertility goddesses and indicate "a bond between the numinous-imaginative and the realm of the spirits and the dead . . ." (*GM*, p. 113). While the Great Mother in her aspect of fertility goddess tends to be characterized by a naturalistic, "sensuous" form, "her aspect as ruler over the spirits and the dead favors forms stressing the unnatural, unreal, and 'spiritual' " (*GM*, p. 108). The sensuous manifestations of the goddess, predominant in Keats's works, denote an extroverted attitude, while her abstract manifestations, present in Poe's and Cortázar's, denote these writers' introverted attitudes and their tendency to identify woman with death.

Somoza, introverted and obsessive, sublimates his desire for Thérèse (his friend's wife and, as such, "taboo") by translating it into the desire to enter the world of the goddess Haghesa, whose statuette he has unearthed. But this goddess is the ruler of the dead; her rituals demand that he become her high priest, the one who will carry out the ritual sacrifices in her honor. Somoza, in his obsession, succumbs to the onrush of "ancestral memories," and gradually abandons his modern identity as he passes into Haghesa's own time. The ancient religions of Asia Minor were never fully suppressed; in the ensuing syncretism, primitive rituals were preserved. Even though Byzantium, the City of the Goddess, became Constantinople, the City of the Virgin, Byzantine priests preserved a terrible, more ancient ritual: the priest's castration in honor of the goddess.[28] Somoza's unconscious "possession" by the spirit of the goddess has, thus, an even darker connotation. Finally, Somoza is transported to a "sacred time" and, having totally surrendered his twentieth-century self, prepares to carry out Morand's sacrifice. The latter, however, kills Somoza in self-defense accomplishing thus the ritual to Haghesa. "Possessed," in his turn, through his active, though unpremeditated participation in the ritual, he assumes the role of sacrificial priest and lies in ambush, awaiting the arrival of his next victim: Thérèse.

"Las ménades" recreates, in a contemporary atmosphere, the ritual killing and dismemberment of the god in the primitive matriarchal rites. As Neumann states, "Death and dismemberment or castration are the fate of the phallus bearing, youthful god . . . both are associated with bloody orgies in the cult of the Great Mother."[29] In this story, the "seasonal King" is the director of the orchestra, the "maenads" his public, who gather in the concert hall in the midst of an atmosphere of increasing heat and excitement. The tension builds up in a masterful *crescendo* that succeeds in involving the reader in the "ritual." At a certain point, a woman in red advances towards the stage, as if in a trance, marking the beginning of the orgy. At the end of the story, a frenzied public destroys the theater and overwhelms the conductor and the members of the orchestra. Finally, the woman in red emerges licking her lips. The motif of the enraged maenads recurs—briefly but effectively—in Cortázar's last novel, *Libro de Manuel*. In it, Oscar—a younger mirror-image of the protagonist, Andrés Fava—suffers from a recurring, obsessive vision: that of the "moonstruck" girls who escape the confinement of a hospital and form what appears to be a society of enraged maenads. Although the apparent intention of this episode is to condemn society's "confining" aspect, likening it to the hospital, the vision seems to have a deeper meaning. Indeed, the whole episode has that indefinable character that marks the situations derived from the author's "archetypal" nightmares and obsessions. When described at first, the episode appears as a frightening vision: the girls escape from the hospital, gather under the moon, run half-naked and half-maddened. Oscar experiences a vague feeling of fright as he remembers his nightmare, which curiously recurs whenever he meets Gladis, with whom he is carrying on a superficial affair. If the dream simply denounces society's confining aspect, why should Oscar, one of the revolutionaries, be disturbed by the girls' flight from that confinement? Evidently, the moonstruck, nearly hysterical girls have more than a merely social symbolism. Their portrayal likens them to the legendary maenads, driven to frenzy and in pursuit of a sacrificial victim. Oscar, unconsciously afraid of Gladis, seems to fear he might be the object of the maenads' pursuit.

A more concrete evidence of Keats's influence is to be found in connection with "La Belle Dame sans Merci" and *Lamia*. The genesis of "La Belle Dame" is enveloped with an aura of mystery that must have presented a special attraction for Cortázar. Keats seems to have conceived the poem in a hypnotic mood, half asleep. The poem was written at an important point in Keats's life; his brother Tom had died shortly before, and he had recently met Fanny Brawne, who was destined to play a crucial role in Keats's life. Several sources for the poem have been pointed out; Gittings sees Burton's *Anatomy of Melancholy*—which Keats read extensively at this time—behind the portrayal of the solitary, melancholy dreamer in the poem.[30] Coleridge's "Christabel"— conceived in a similar mood—presents an analogous mysterious atmosphere where legend blends with nightmare. Moreover, the story of Tom Keats's own infatuation with the fictitious "Amena" of the love letters seems to have been in the back of Keats's mind. Keats—who had received the packet of "Amena's" letters shortly before—was convinced that this painful episode had contributed to accelerate his brother's death. But behind all these influences, there remains an unexplained element that can only be related to the archetypal roots of the story. As Robert Gittings adequately observes, none of these influences can account for "the intensity and underlying depth of a poem which brought Keats's darkest and most fundamental experiences to the surface."[31]

"La Belle Dame" presents that significant blend of characteristics from the A− and M− characters of the archetype in the previously discussed Schema II. The image we encounter at the beginning of the poem is that of the forsaken, lonely youth already smitten with a deadly "disease":

> I see a lilly on thy brow,
> With anguish moist and fever dew;
> And on thy cheeks a fading rose
> Fast withereth too.

(ll. 9-12)

The cause of the disease is linked to the mysterious lady the knight has met in the meads. Her description is hallowed with the supernatural aura distinctive of all manifestations of the archetype of the Magna Mater. The lady is

> Full beautiful−a faery's child,
> Her hair was long, her foot was light,
> And her eyes were wild.

(ll. 14-16)

She completely absorbs his senses ("And nothing else [the knight] saw all day long," l. 22), and keeps him in subjection by means of magical foods and drinks (ll. 25-26). By closing her eyes with "kisses four," the knight is not merely displaying a common manifestation of love, but he is performing a symbolic action whereby he "shuts her eyes" as well as his own to the reality beyond the "elfin grot." Likewise, the line "she lulled me asleep" (l. 33) possesses the connotation of a spiritual, as well as a physical, slumber and foreshadows the sleep of death that haunts the knight as we encounter him at the beginning of the poem. In the dream, the knight sees

> . . . pale kings and princes too,
> Pale warriors, death-pale were they all;
> They cried−"La Belle Dame sans Merci
> Hath thee in thrall!"

(ll. 37-40)

The vision of the Belle Dame's victims, appearing to him "with horrid warning" (l. 42), makes the knight realize the horror of his condition: he is asleep, blind, and under the subjection of a sorceress who will drain the life away from his body. At that very moment both lady and grot disappear, and the knight finds himself "palely loitering," forsaken and alone, as the poem returns to the setting of the opening stanzas.

As I previously observed, the Belle Dame possesses a deadly character that, transcending the qualities of the negative anima, could identify her with the archetypal Terrible Mother, whose function it is to extinguish consciousness and take back to herself, through death, that which had attempted to break away from her domination. In this poem, Cortázar saw an externalization of his own feelings towards women. We can hear echoes of this poem in several of his later creations. A noticeable parallel is to be found between "La Belle Dame" and Cortázar's story "Cuello de gatito negro," published in *Octaedro*.

Cortázar's story blends in itself characteristics from both Keats's "La Belle Dame" and the episode of Diana and Actaeon from Ovid's *Metamorphoses*. Lucho, whose name is reminiscent of Lycius, the hero in *Lamia*, finds the weeping Dina, apparently by chance, in one of his journeys in the Paris metro. The solitary mead of "La Belle Dame," the forest of *Lamia*, and the grove of Ovid's story have their modern counterpart in a tunnel of the Paris metro; though less poetic, the metro retains the characteristic aspect of "isolation" of the other settings, since it is "underground" and dark. Moreover, the train is usually associated, in Cortázar's works (let us remember the tramways in the nightmares of *62*), with the laws of chance ruling every decisive or numinous encounter. Juan, fascinated by Dina, and particularly by Dina's hands, follows her to her apartment—the modern counterpart of the "elfin grot." There, they taste the pleasures of sensuality. But soon afterwards, Dina shows her "terrible" aspect: her hands, acquiring a life of their own, pull at his penis and attempt to scratch his eyes out. At the end of the story, he stands alone in the hallway, cold, naked, pale, and confused, like the youth in Keats's poem. Cortázar's story emphasizes, much more than Keats's poem, the "terrible" aspect of the enchantress. Keats's poem merely hints at the death the knight is to suffer by presenting the Belle Dame's victims in the knight's dream; but she is never portrayed explicitly in her "terrible" manifestation. Cortázar's story, on the other hand, presents the total reversal of the shy, weeping Dina into the fierce, bloodthirsty Black Artemis. Dina's name is very similar to the name Diana; Diana's "dark" manifestation appears in Ovid's story, where the goddess, avenging herself for Actaeon's entrance into her sacred grove and his looking at her naked body, turns him into an animal and has him torn to pieces by his own mastifs. The Terrible Diana was represented as a Black Goddess; Dina, a native of Martinique, is dark-skinned. Moreover, as in Ovid's story, Lucho looks at Dina without "seeing" her, just as Actaeon had looked at Diana's body without recognizing her divine nature. Lucho's "blindness" is symbolically alluded to in the reference to the lamp Dina unsuccessfully attempts to light, being impeded by Lucho's repeated amatory demands. Finally, Lucho breaks the lamp as she reaches for it. In the ensuing darkness, Dina turns into an aggressive maenad, attempting to blind and castrate Lucho.

The presence of *Lamia* can be detected behind Cortázar's best-known novels, *Rayuela* and *62*. The ambiguousness implied in the character of the Belle Dame, who represents both Love and Death, is more explicit in the character of the lamia. It has been rightly observed that the symbol of the lamia is especially attractive to Keats, since it permits him to embody the mingled attraction and repulsion characteristic of his treatment of woman as a love object.[32] Indeed, Lamia represents both the ideal goddess and the dream lover that Lycius, a dreamer, had longed for. But in *Lamia* Keats employs an ironic tone that was absent from "La Belle Dame." If in the latter Keats had presented the knight's doom objectively, without attempting to blame it on the weaknesses in the knight's character, in *Lamia* he seems to adopt a critical position regarding his protagonist's attitude and, indeed, regarding his former poetic self. *Lamia* belongs to a period in Keats's development when he was trying to develop an "Apollinian" outlook to counteract his basically "Dionysiac" nature. In *The Fall of Hyperion: A Dream*—which also belongs to this period—he had established a differentiation between the poet (the one who accepts his link to a specific human group and tries to alleviate their sufferings through his art) and the dreamer (the selfish visionary who rejects the world for the sake of his ideal visions). By presenting Lycius as a "dreamer" and making him die at the end of the poem, he seems to be trying to "exorcize" Lycius' attitude in himself.[33] Keats is very much in control of this aspect of the poem's symbolism, even if his conception of the lamia undergoes a radical metamorphosis in the course of the poem; every element in it contributes to prepare the reader for the final outcome.

In the initial section of the poem, Lamia is presented as the beautiful, cruel seductress who ensnares the unwary dreamer by means of her magical crafts; yet, there is also a mockery, on Keats's part, of the naiveté with which Lycius succumbs to her traps. Lycius had gone to the temple of Cenchreae to offer a sacrifice to Jove and meets Lamia on his way back from it; apparently, he seems to have asked Jove for a happy marriage, for we read that "Jove heard his vows and better'd his desire" (I, l. 229). Lycius, a scholar, is so concerned with his ideal visions that he even misses the concretion of his own desires when he passes her on the road. He had been wearied with his companions' talk and walked alone, abandoning himself to his fantasies without any interruption from the outside world:

> Over the solitary hills he fared,
> Thoughtless at first, but ere eve's star appeared
> His phantasy was lost, where reason fades,
> In the calm'd twilight of Platonic shades,
> Lamia beheld him coming, near, more near—
> Close to her passing, in indifference drear,
> His silent sandals swept the mossy green;
> So neighbour'd to him and yet so unseen

> She stood: he pass'd, shut up in mysteries,
> His mind wrapp'd like his mantle . . .
>
> (I, ll. 233-42)

Even though Lycius is a scholar, his fantasy prevails over his reason; Lycius' reason "fades" as he is lost in nocturnal fantasies or "Platonic shades." Keats emphasizes Lycius' "blindness" when confronting the objectification of the ideal vision he longed for: Lamia stands "so neighbour'd to him, and yet so unseen"; his mind, "wrapp'd like his mantle," is so totally turned inwards that he fails to notice the presence of that "nymph" for whom he apparently longed. However, when he finally notices Lamia, he does not doubt for a second that she is a goddess sent in answer to his desires. He accepts her as such without further questioning, looking at her, "not with cold wonder fearingly / But Orpheus-like at an Eurydice" (I, ll. 247-48). The mention of Orpheus has ironic overtones, for Orpheus loses his beloved when he "looks" at her, just as Lycius will lose Lamia towards the end of the poem. Keats's ironic treatment of Lycius is sustained throughout the first part of the poem; Lycius soon forgets the goddess for the sake of the woman:

> . . . gentle Lamia judg'd, and judg'd aright
> That Lycius could not love in half a fright,
> So threw the goddess off, and won his heart
> More pleasantly by playing woman's part.
>
> (I, ll. 334-37)

Absorbed in his passion for the being whom he sees as the concretion of his ideals, he appears as a ludicrous, gullible figure: "Lycius to all made eloquent reply / Marrying to every word a twinborn sigh" (I, ll. 340-41). He is not even aware that Lamia has shortened the way to Corinth from three leagues to a few paces; her trick is "not at all surmised / By blinded Lycius, so in her comprized" (I, ll. 346-47).

Even though Keats portrays Lamia as a snake *travesti*, an evil creature responsible for his hero's destruction, she is not presented as a totally repulsive character. Although her cruelty is evinced by the calm premeditation with which she makes Lycius swoon by threatening him with the withdrawal of her affections (I, ll. 286-95), her love for Lycius, later in the poem, makes her surrender her supernatural powers and please Lycius by her charms as woman only. Unlike the Belle Dame, who rends her lovers and then forsakes them, Lamia submits to Lycius and remains beside him. The tragic outcome of the poem is indirectly blamed on Lycius.

Like the ecstasy Circe provided, the pleasure Lamia offers Lycius is one-sided; it is a happiness that excludes every thought of reality. Lamia had the ability "to unperplex bliss from its neighbor pain" (I, l. 192). She, a supernatural being, is capable of enjoying an undisturbed kind of happiness isolated

from worldly cares; he, a human, must feel "the strife of opposites." Lycius
soon tires of Lamia's unworldly bliss and longs to return to the world, for

> Love in a palace is perhaps at last
> More grievous torment than a hermit's fast:—
>
> (II, ll. 3-4)

As Lycius listens to the sounds of trumpets outside the palace, he is reminded
of "the noisy world almost forsworn" (II, l. 33) and attempts to convince
Lamia to leave the palace and announce their love to the rest of the world. As
Lamia, grown weak and frightened at the thought of losing Lycius, pleads
with him, trying to change his mind, his behavior towards her takes a sadistic
turn. The initial relationship is now reversed:

> . . . she nothing said, but pale and meek,
> Arose and knelt before him, wept a rain
> Of sorrows at his words; at last with pain
> Beseeching him, the while his hand she wrung,
> To change his purpose. He thereat was stung,
> Perverse, with stronger fancy to reclaim
> Her wild and timid nature to his aim:
> Besides, for all his love, in self despite,
> Against his better self, he took delight
> Luxurious in her sorrows, soft and new.
> His passion, cruel grown, took on a hue
> Fierce and sanguineous as 'twas possible
> In one whose brow had no dark veins to swell.
>
> (II, ll. 65-77)

Cortázar's comments on the above lines are very revealing; he observes that
Lycius' attitude towards Lamia, in Part II of the poem, constitutes "un
comportamiento de la más alta importancia" (*IJK*, p. 277). He terms this
behavior "sadismo poético," stating that it constitutes a method whose aim
it is to attain the ontological possession of its object (*IJK*, p. 277). According
to Cortázar, the poet possesses reality by means of analogies, through meta-
phors that link unfamiliar objects with the familiar ones they resemble. Only
contraries, those objects that possess no analogy to one another, escape the
poet's tendency to embrace them in one central metaphor and must be appre-
hended separately. According to Cortázar, Keats felt anguished and even angered
at his inability to conciliate opposites in his heart and in his mind, and he
cites the "Epistle to Reynolds" as an exemplification of those feelings, adding:
"Que el día no sea también la noche lo aterra y lo encoleriza; que cada cosa
aprehendida presuponga su contrario remoto e inalcanzable lo humilla" (*IJK*,
p. 277). Keats's answer to this schism, he continues, is expressed in a gesture
that embraces opposites in a higher form of oneness. If there is no real analogy

between two objects or feelings, the poet invents it; thus, Keats conceives of the expression "pleasant pain" as he solves the mystery of polarization by his *acceptance of opposites* (*IJK*, p. 277).

Most of Keats's critics would agree with Cortázar's interpretation of the expression "pleasant pain" and with his appreciation of Keats's sensitivity to polarizations.[34] His use of the term "method of poetic sadism," however, is questionable. Cortázar implies that Keats deliberately introduced the element of sadism in the poem in order to embrace, in a broader concept, the contradictory emotions love arouses. However, the very conception of a *"method* for an ontological possession of reality" (Cortázar's terminology) is alien to Keats's nature. The use of a "method" implies the preconception of a system of abstractions that is then applied to a concrete situation. It presupposes a certain distance and controlled coldness on the subject's part regarding the object of his attention. Yet abstract thinking, in the ordinary sense, was alien to Keats; as Murry observes, "the movement of his thought was richly imaged, and amazingly concrete—'sensations rather than thoughts.' "[35] I do not believe Keats's attitude in *Lamia* evinces the cool, controlled distance the use of a preconceived method would betray. The poem's ambiguousness regarding the lamia and Lycius undermines the theory that Keats was working according to a "method of poetic sadism."

The concept of "poetic sadism," in its assumption of a preconceived method, actually applies to Poe's stories better than to *Lamia*. In any case, Cortázar's reading of *Lamia* gives us an important clue for the interpretation of certain episodes in *Rayuela*, where a "method of poetic sadism" seems to be, indeed, at work.

Lamia ends with the death of Lycius as the lamia fades away under the gaze of the philosopher Apollonius. Keats had meant, apparently, to exorcize his former fascination with "ideal beauty" of an unreal kind and condemn his former pursuit of the idyllic bower. Yet he is unable to make his hero return to the claims of "reality"; Lycius dies once the lamia disappears. One might say that she appears as the archetypal Terrible Mother, who ensnares her victims to such a degree that they cannot survive the withdrawal of her affection.

The first part of *Rayuela* presents a number of parallels with both "La Belle Dame" and *Lamia*. According to Professor Barrenechea—who possesses the working notebooks for *Rayuela*—one of the first chapters originally conceived in this novel was the one that later became Chapter 123 in Part III. In it Oliveira returns to a scene of his childhood; there, he sees his sister, the garden, the house of his childhood days. Upon awakening, he is invaded by the feeling that the dream had a far greater "reality" than anything else he had later experienced; the reality of the room in Paris and la Maga's company appeared to be, indeed, the dream. From the beginning, then, Cortázar sees the character of la Maga as "unreal," illusory, the figment of imagination, or of a dream—like the lamia or the Belle Dame. Moreover, Oliveira, like Lycius and the knight, is more of a dreamer than a poet, and as such, one who "venoms all his days" and "vexes the world," rather than one who "pours a balm" on it. Like Lycius, Horacio is seen, at the beginning of the novel (if we choose the "hopscotch" way of reading and begin with Chapter 73) lost in his mental speculations. Like the knight (if we choose the "normal" way of reading and begin with Chapter 1), he wanders about, "palely loitering," searching for the ideal woman, the enchantress who has captivated his senses and then abandoned him. Just as Lycius's search for "ideal forms" finds a concrete expression in his obsession with the supernatural Lamia, so Oliveira's metaphysical longings find a concrete expression in his desire to enter la Maga's world. The Belle Dame is presented as "a faery's child"; the transformation of the lamia into the woman and the duality of her nature are presented at the very beginning of Keats's poems. La Maga is presented as a concrete woman with a good share of all-too-human stupidity; yet, the author clothes her with a supernatural aura that is many times stressed throughout the novel.

From the beginning, la Maga is presented as an elusive, mysterious female who, as "anima," entices the hero to adventure. Her description is unmistakably "unreal": we read about "su delgada cintura" and "su fina cara de translúcida piel" (*R*, p. 15). Moreover, her very name is deliberately symbolic: la Maga's name is Lucía, that is, "she who has the light"; Oliveira gives her the epithet that identifies her both with Circe and with the symbolic figure in the second mystery of the Tarot. "La Maga"—or the Archpriestess—is Isis, goddess of the night: "She is seated, holding a half-opened book in her right hand and two keys in her left, one of which is golden (signifying the sun, the work, or reason) and the other silver (the moon or imagination). . . . She is leaning against the sphinx of the great cosmic questions, and the floor, being composed of alternate white and black tiles, denotes that everything in existence is subject to the laws of chance and of opposites."[36] Isis, as Archpriestess and Moon Goddess, has been traditionally associated with the esoteric rites of initiation, from Apuleius' *The Golden Ass* to Godfrey Higgins' *Anacalypsis*. In Jungian theory, Isis, a representative of the Magna Mater, is identical with Ishtar of Babylonia, Astarte of Phoenicia, Kali-Durga and Anna-Purna of India, Demeter in Greece, and Themis in Asia Minor. But, most importantly, Isis is the figure that best exemplifies the triple aspect of the Magna Mater as inspiration, Good-Bad Mother, and Terrible Mother.

La Maga is also alluded to with another of the Magna Mater's names, that of the Great Whore of Babylonia: "nos fuimos a tomar una copa de *pelure d'oignon* a un café de Sèvres-Babylone (hablando de metáforas, yo delicada porcelana recién desembarcada, HANDLE WITH CARE, y ella Babilonia, raíz de tiempo, cosa anterior, *primeval being*, terror y delicia de los comienzos, romanticismo de Atalá pero con un tigre auténtico esperando detrás del árbol)" (*R*, p. 486). The presence of the baby Rocamadour, named after the French Virgin of Rocamadour, further implies an identification of la Maga with the archetypal Virgin Mother, another aspect of the Magna Mater. As Dr. Esther Harding remarks, the word "Virgin," that gives name to one of the twelve constellations of the Zodiac, did not have, for the ancients, the value it has today; it alluded to a psychological, rather than to a physical, condition. A physical virgin was called a "virgo intacta," while the word "virgo" itself was specifically used to designate a woman who "possessed herself" and did not cling to any particular man or demand that his relationship to her be permanent. Such a woman could be a "virgo" whether or not she was a mother and whether her behavior was exemplary or licentious.[37]

In any case, la Maga—in spite of the numerous rapes she is subjected to— retains an oddly ascetic aura about her. The love scenes between her and Oliveira are actually rape scenes; it is in the scenes with Pola that we find more balanced erotic encounters. Pola, though far more "concrete" than la Maga, is also identified with one of the symbolic attributes of the Magna Mater: the City. As Pola-Paris she appears as the Earth, or the provider of sensuous pleasure, while la Maga-Isis appears primarily as the subject of inspiration. La Maga, as agent of transformation, performs the role of "anima"[38] through the first eight chapters in the novel. Yet even though la Maga first appears as anima, Oliveira does not succumb totally to her attraction. In fact, he appears like a forewarned Lycius, a Lycius who has read "La Belle Dame sans Merci" and *Lamia*. While Keats's heroes lose themselves in the intensity of their passions, Oliveira remains coolly detached and suspicious. On the other hand, in spite of the initial bliss he seems to experience with la Maga, he can never abandon himself completely to the full intensity of passion ("éramos como dos músicos," etc.), apparently from fear of being completely absorbed and lost in the world of la Maga. Like Lycius, Horacio feels he must go on to something else; unlike Lamia, la Maga offers no resistance to his desire to live his own life and engage in concerns other than herself. In fact, Oliveira is seldom presented in la Maga's company, except in the erotic scenes. Most often he is with the members of the Club, with or without la Maga, or with his other mistress, Pola, with whom he has an affair with the knowledge and apparent consent of la Maga. As Oliveira feels the call of the outside world, from which he fears la Maga will separate him, he resorts to a sadistic behavior against her, just as Lycius had regarding Lamia. Yet their perverseness is, essentially, of a different nature. In Keats's poem, perverseness appears as an amplification of the concept of love that includes suffering as well as joy; it explores a new aspect of Lycius' relationship to Lamia (Lycius takes delight in her sorrows, "soft and *new*"). Oliveira's cruelty towards la Maga, on the other hand, seems to respond, indeed, to what Cortázar termed a "method of poetic sadism" in his discussion of *Lamia*. Oliveira's cruelty is cold, even premeditated and objective. Its chief object seems to be *Oliveira's self-defense*, and the preservation of his identity in the face of the mounting threat posed by la Maga. As in Poe's stories ("Berenice," "The Fall of the House of Usher,"

"The Oval Portrait," "The Black Cat"), the hero paradoxically expresses his love through the destruction of its object, thus freeing himself from the manic states and the anxiety neuroses provoked by the object of his love. Just as Egaeus' love for Berenice increases as the heroine sickens and is on the verge of death, and just as Roderick Usher's love for his sister Madeline finds its extreme expression in the entombment of his live sister in a crypt while she is under the effects of a cataleptic seizure, Oliveira's love increases with la Maga's sorrows, and his highest expression of love is manifested in his desertion of la Maga after the death of her child. If we attribute what Cortázar calls a "method of poetic sadism" to Cortázar's own works, the reason for Oliveira's behavior becomes clear. According to this declaration, the author wishes to burst through the usual demarcations and definitions of "love" and "hatred" by presenting a situation that encompasses both. Such had been the effect attained by Keats in *Lamia*. But in *Rayuela* the author's overt intention seems too noticeable, and moreover, we seem to detect a more subtle and unconscious force below the surface. That "hidden force" seems to be the hero's desire to protect himself from the devastating effect of passion: the dissolution of the self. The dread of the "devouring" female is, as we have seen, an important theme in Cortázar's works from the very beginning, and it had played a central role in his two preceding novels, *El examen* and *Los premios*. *Rayuela* is the work where it is first openly confronted and portrayed; the author has brought himself to a point where he attempts to dissect the relationship between his hero and heroine, yet fears to carry the "operation" to its utmost conclusions.

If in *Lamia* and "La Belle Dame" the sorceress abandons the hero, here it is Oliveira who first leaves la Maga on the night of the baby Rocamadour's death; when she later leaves the apartment, it is because he has indirectly ordered her to do so. Yet, as soon as she leaves, Oliveira literally falls apart, expressing his longing for her. If the knight in "La Belle Dame" has the mark of death on his brow and cheeks after the sorceress deserts him and Lycius collapses dead on the point of Lamia's disappearance, Oliveira becomes progressively weakened throughout the second part of the novel, but the final outcome is the same as in Keats's poems. Even though Oliveira originally intended to desert la Maga in order to preserve his freedom and pursue his literary ambitions, after she leaves he betrays that very freedom by setting up housekeeping with the foolish Gekrepten and nearly abandons all literary concerns, absorbed by the haunting memory of la Maga. Once his defense system is thoroughly broken (after the episode in the morgue, where he "accepts" la Maga in Talita's person), he faces three possible destinies: madness, suicide, or symbolic castration through his subjection to the motherly Gekrepten. Various critics and the author himself have claimed that the novel has an "open ending" and that Oliveira's future has endless possibilities. I believe, however, that we must limit ourselves to what is expressed in the text itself. And the text offers only these three possibilities, all of which imply a dissolution of the self, an overturning of the mind that is the archetypal outcome of an encounter with the Terrible Mother, as has been exemplified in our analysis of both of Keats's poems.

Even though the "terrible" side of la Maga is merely hinted at in the episode involving her spell on Pola, her nature is known through the effect she provokes on Horacio; the novel, thus, presents an ideal case of negative anima projection, since the heroine is not objectively presented as a wicked sorceress but is mostly known to us through the effects she has wrought on Oliveira. There is, however, another indirect allusion to la Maga's "terrible" aspect in the second part of the novel: the references to "el perro." The references to "the dog" first appear towards the end of the novel, soon before Oliveira's encounter with the ghost of la Maga in the asylum's morgue. As the asylum is transferred to a new owner—the former director of the circus—the patients are asked to sign the deed signifying their consent in order to legalize the transaction. The patients, however, demand the death of a dog as a necessary condition before they grant approval. No further explanations are given; "the dog" remains a cryptic allusion that gains an ominous aura as it is reiterated. Dogs are a symbol of the Terrible Mother and are associated with the "tearing to pieces" symbolic of madness and dissolution of the self through the fragmentation of the personality. Diana's dogs tear Actaeon to pieces in revenge for his having looked at her without seeing her. Dogs are also the companions of Hecate, identified with Artemis in Greek syncretism and, in fact, Artemis' "dark" aspect. "El perro" can be interpreted, then, as an objectification of Oliveira's dread of la Maga's return, and of the fragmentation of his consciousness through the shock occasioned by that return. This is, actually, what happens at the end of the novel; and the references to "the dog" act, then, as a premonition. The symbol of the dog reappears in Cortázar's next novel, *62: Modelo para armar*, where the archetype of the Terrible Mother is further elaborated.

The character of Hélène holds a greater direct affinity with the lamia and the Belle Dame. Firstly, both heroines are associated with the mythical figure of the vampire and with Hecate, the "dark" Moon Goddess, ruler of the underworld, witchcraft, madness, and death. That Lamia and Hélène both represent the "spook" Moon Goddess Hecate—traditionally associated with witches, phantoms, and vampires (cf. Schema II above)—can be confirmed by recalling Hecate's traditional attributes: "As an incubus or vampire she [Hecate] appears in the form of Empusa, or as a man-eating lamia, or again in that more beautiful guise, the 'Bride of Corinth.' "[39] Lamia is, concretely, the "Bride of Corinth," whose story, derived from Philostratus' *Life of Apollonius of Tyana*, Keats found in Burton's *Anatomy of Melancholy*; Hélène, who lives in the rue de la Clef, possesses "the key," one of Hecate's traditional attributes, together with the torch and the dog.[40] Both are, thus, identified as vampiresses, as man-eating lamiae.

Cortázar confirms the identification of Hélène with the "terrible" side of the Moon Goddess further in the novel. Juan, who had called Hélène "a basilisk" (a variation of the vampire), also identifies her with Diana. On the night of their encounter, Juan tells Hélène: "Siempre me tuviste rencor, siempre te vengaste de alguna manera. ¿Quieres saber cómo me llamó un día mi paredro? Acteón" (*62*, p. 235). Later, she tells him:

> Vaya a saber si Diana no se entregó a Acteón, pero lo que cuenta es que *después le echó los perros* y probablemente gozó viendo como lo destrozaban. No soy Diana *pero siento que en alguna parte de mí hay perros que esperan*, y no hubiera querido que te hicieran pedazos. (*62*, p. 238; my italics)

If the relationship between "el perro" and the Terrible Mother aspect in la Maga had been merely suggested in *Rayuela*, it becomes explicit—as the preceding quotation démonstrates—in the case of Hélène. Like la Maga in the second part of *Rayuela*, Hélène seems to be motivated by a vague desire for *revenge*.

Like Lycius, Juan is manipulated by forces he can neither understand nor control. He tries to find sensuous oblivion through his relationship with Tell and attempts to "blur his vision" through constant drinking (we never see Juan without a drink in his hands—Campari, whiskey, slivovitz, Médoc, Sylvaner . . .). Juan is in love with a symbol: the petrified and petrifying beauty of the Medusa, Empusa Hélène, the evasive anesthetist of the rue de la Clef. Juan's monologues stress Hélène's unreal nature from the very beginning; he says: "¿Estabas en la zona o te soñé? . . . Pero tú, Hélène, ¿habrás sido una vez más un nombre que levanto contra la nada, el simulacro que me invento con palabras . . . ?" (*62*, p. 21). Later, we realize that, unlike Lycius, Juan does not want Hélène "to throw the goddess off"; in fact, he loves her *as goddess*, precisely because of her evasiveness and coldness: "Hélène Arp, Hélène Brancusi, . . . fría astuta indiferente crueldad cortés de infanta entre suplicantes y enanos . . . (La sombra de Hélène es más densa que las otras y más fría; quien posa el pie en sus sargazos siente subir el veneno que lo hará vivir para siempre en el único delirio necesario). . ." (*62*, pp. 76-77). Even though he suspects Hélène's true nature, Juan *does not want to face it*; at the end of the novel we read: ". . . te quería demasiado para aceptar esa alucinación en la que ni siquiera estabas presente . . . llegué al borde y preferí no saber, consentí en no saber aunque hubiera podido . . ." (*62*, p. 262).

Like Lycius, Juan becomes obsessed with his vampiress, almost disregarding the rest of the world. Both heroes, however, really succumb to the destructiveness of *their own* passions, rather than to an innate perfidy on the part of the beloved. Just as Lamia, the "cruel lady" of the opening scenes, becomes tame and submissive as the poem progresses, and she seems to have become truly human through her love for Lycius, so Hélène displays at least a desire to become "human" on the night of her encounter with Juan: she obsessively wipes her face as if trying to remove a mask (*62*, p. 237), and she asks Juan to change her, if he can (*62*, p. 238). Neither Keats nor Cortázar succeeds in presenting the heroine as a truly repulsive creature (in spite of the explicit identification of the heroine with the snake and the vampire, respectively) because each author seems to place a great part of the blame on the hero himself; he does not love the woman but the dream, and by rejecting the real for the sake of the ideal vision, he succumbs under the weight of the reality he was unwilling to face, once the object of his fantasy disappears. Lycius asks the gods for a dream woman; once his wish is granted, he wants to impose his dream on the diurnal world and is destroyed by his folly. Juan, likewise, wants to love *his own* Hélène, and thus provokes her wrath when he unwittingly refuses to see her "unmasked" face (*62*, p. 262).

As is always the case when the hero "turns away" from an archetype arising from his disconcerted psyche, the refusal of the archetype's summons turns the adventure into a negative one. Rather than being saved, the hero becomes doomed; all he can do is await the process of his disintegration. The hero refuses to give up his present dreams and ideals, for he sees the future not as a process of growth, but as an indefinite prolongation of his present state; hence, he becomes imprisoned in his infantile ego, unable to make the passage from his inner world to the world outside. His former "dream vision" becomes a monster that will constantly haunt him; his very house, a house of death.

2

Woman as Death

In the preface he wrote to his translation of Poe's prose works, Cortázar acknowledges Hervey Allen's *Israfel* and Arthur Hobson Quinn's *Edgar Allan Poe* as his main sources of information. And so they are in matters regarding the major external events in Poe's life. Yet, when reducing Quinn's 750 pages and Allen's 700 to fit the 50 pages of the introduction, Cortázar has naturally been selective in his choice of information. He certainly felt he had earned the right—after two years of close contact with Poe—to give us his own interpretation of certain major events in Poe's life. There are isolated passages in Cortázar's introduction to Poe's works where he departs from a factual, detached style in order to present the details gathered from Allen's and Quinn's biographies and adopts an attitude where he displays a sympathetic identification with Poe. These passages are invariably linked—in the biographical section—to Poe's relationship to women; in them, we see the "chameleon" at work.

Cortázar's biographical foreword to his translation of Poe's works underscores Poe's reaction to his stepfather's infidelities, which had resulted in an indefinite number of illegitimate offspring. Poe's biographers usually minimize the emotional impact this discovery made on Poe, while emphasizing the material worries it later gave rise to, as Poe came to realize the precariousness of his position regarding John Allan. But Cortázar underplays the material shock, stressing Poe's feeling of outrage at the insult that had been perpetrated against his (step)mother: "Parece seguro que su primera reacción contra Allan nació de su cólera por la ofensa que ese descubrimiento infería a Frances. También ésta lo supo y debió de confiarse a Edgar, que tomó resueltamente su partido."[1] (*OP*, p. XXII). Thus, Cortázar brings to the fore the antagonistic nature of the relationship between father and son, while presenting Edgar, in a way, as the "knight" who defends his "abandoned" mother. This comment suddenly becomes enlightening if we consider that Cortázar's interpretation of the episode recreates a situation associated with the central "constellation" in his psyche: that of Parsifal and his mother.

Further in his preface, Cortázar displays a truer chameleonism when he apprehends the basic constellation of the Feminine in Poe and his discussion of the poet's infatuation with Mrs. Jane Stith Stanard, "Helen." Indeed, the archetypal Helen, Helen of Troy, seems to have embodied the latent archetype of the Feminine in Poe's unconscious; he had vague memories of his beautiful actress-mother, who came and went whither he knew not, elaborately dressed and made-up, and one day disappeared forever. Later, as he studied mythology, the figure of Helen of Troy seems to have crystal-lized his vague memories of the first feminine presence in his life, and the name "Helen" became, for him, the epitome of beauty . . . but also of danger. For Helen possesses a dual aspect: she is both the ideal figure, the epitomi-zation of beauty, inspiring and forever unattainable, and, on the other hand, the Fatal Woman, who, as agent of death and destruction, came to occupy the Romantic imagination during the latter part of the nineteenth century.[2] "Helen" became Poe's favorite name; when he met Mrs. Stanard, his ideal con-cept found a corporeal manifestation, "and there need be no explanation necessary of his change from Mrs. Stanard's own first name."[3] "To Helen"—the poem Poe dedicated to her—expresses perhaps better than any other the poet's characteristic longing for the perfect presence of woman as guide and inspira-tion—in short, as anima. Poe saw "Helen" as a goddess among mortals, and loved to watch her stately figure moving softly through the house, lighting the lamps at dusk and emerging from the shadows as she went. And like his mother, Helen disappeared one day; to quote only one of his biographers, "like his own mother, she appeared to him briefly, a vision, and then was taken away from him. She became an ideal, the epitomization of beauty, unattainable and forever identified with death."[4]

If most of Poe's biographers consider the "Helen" episode as the most decisive in Poe's youth, Cortázar goes one step further and interprets it as the crucial episode *in his life*, as the moment in which Poe first confronted his deeper self and expressed "su primera aceptación del destino que habría de signar toda su vida":

> "Helen" es la primera mujer—en una larga galería—de quien Edgar Poe habría de enamorarse *sabiendo* que era un ideal, sólo un ideal, y enamorarse *porque* era ese ideal y no meramente una mujer conquistable. . . . El adolescente que acudía a casa de su condiscípulo sin otro propósito que el de jugar, fue recibido por la Musa. . . . Ignorándolo, "Helen" le exigió que ingresara definitivamente en la dimensión de los hombres. Edgar aceptó, enamorándose. Su amor fue secreto, per-fecto, y duró lo que su vida, por debajo o por encima de muchos otros. (*OP*, pp. XXI-XXII; his italics)

If Cortázar had formerly seen "Circe" as the basic constellation of the Feminine in Keats's works, he now sees "Helen" as the basic manifestation of the Femi-nine in Poe's unconscious that will determine his relationships to women and his fictional presentation of them. He states that Poe fell in love with Helen *precisely because* she was an impossible, and not just a mere "conquerable," woman; she was the Muse, the only source of inspiration, the one who, in a way, gave him "permission" to grow up and become a man. He implies—however—that Poe returned her favors by loving *her alone*. Thus, even though Cortázar himself does not state at this point what further developments this basic constellation will determine, his own statements imply that if Helen was the one who "allowed" Poe to become a man, she was also the one who could retire her favors at any moment—and thus take his manhood, his independence, and his very being back upon herself. "Helen," thus, contains in herself attributes that go beyond those of the mere positive or even negative anima; in her aspects of Terrible Mother, Helen's successive transformations will identify her with death, with madness, and with the dissolution of the self.

Cortázar remains faithful to his method of interpretation when dealing with the much later "Helen," Mrs. Sarah Helen Whitman, who became Poe's fiancée after Virginia Clemm's death: "Y entonces entra en escena la etérea Sarah Helen Whitman, poetisa mediocre pero mujer llena de inmaterial encanto, como las heroínas de los mejores sueños vividos o imaginados por Edgar, y que además se llamaba Helen, como él había llamado a su primer amor de adolescencia" (*OP*, p. XLVIII). And truly Cortázar does not exaggerate when he describes Poe's affair with Helen Whitman in these terms; indeed, it seems that Poe fell in love with her, firstly, because her name was "Helen" and thus reminded him of the ideal beloved he carried in his bosom (he hardly knew Mrs. Whitman when he wrote the second "To Helen" for her)[5] and, secondly, because, since she was basically "immaterial," he was free to project his own ideal visions on her. The idyllic nature of his love for "Helen" is patent in the poem he dedicated to her. "To Helen" is generally considered as far inferior to the first "To Helen" (for Mrs. Stanard) or to the later "To Annie" (for Mrs. Nancy Richmond) and "Annabel Lee" (for the deceased Virginia), or even to the poem Poe dedicated to his dear friend Marie Louise Shew, who had watched over Virginia in her agony. Yet, Cortázar stresses one important aspect of Poe's relationship to this second "Helen": his fear of her *possessiveness*. Both Helens were *older* women and, thus, closer to the maternal archetype than to that of the anima (Mrs. Whitman was a well-preserved forty-five when she met Poe, her junior by ten years). But if Mrs. Stanard had been only the protective, inspiring figure, Mrs. Whitman, in her constant supervision of Poe and her distrust of his motives for desiring to marry her, and mostly in her scenes of jealousy regarding his friendship with "Annie," will display for the captive yet rebellious Poe the negative side of the archetype associated with absorption and engulfment. If Helen's attitude was, indeed, "motherly" (she and her mother, Mrs. Powers, supervised Poe's drinking habits like strict disciplinarians), Poe's was, to say the least, complying.

Later, after she had finally broken her engagement to Poe, Mrs. Whitman con-
fessed that she was relieved at "being freed from the intolerable burden of
responsibility which he had sought to impose upon me, by persuading me that
his fate, for good or evil, depended upon *me*."[6]

Poe, who had been a rather "independent" person in his younger years,
traveling alone through several states and perhaps (the legend has never been
truly disproven) throughout Europe, developed an acute anxiety neurosis
in his later years; he could not be alone, away from Virginia *and* Mrs. Clemm.
After Virginia's death, his condition took a turn for the worse; he even needed
Mrs. Clemm to hold his hand at night until he fell asleep. As Cortázar states:
"Lejos de ella, lejos de alguien que lo acompañara y cuidara, Edgar estaba
siempre perdido. El más solitario de los hombres no sabía estar solo" (*OP*,
p. LI).[7] Cortázar stresses at several points in his preface Poe's need for the
feminine presence, but for the feminine *as mother figure*, as the one who
receives, forgives, and protects. At one point, he observes that his pride and
his aura of demonism arose from a basic weakness and from a feeling of
inferiority; only women would know of his weaker moments. With women, he
had no need to impress or pretend; he needed their love and care, *not* their
understanding:

> El hombre que se dispone a escribir es orgulloso, pero su orgullo nace de una
> esencial debilidad que se ha refugiado, como el cangrejo ermitaño, en una caracola
> de violencia luciferina, de arrebato incontenible. El cangrejo Poe sólo abandona la
> valva de su orgullo frente a sus seres queridos, sus poquísimos seres queridos.
> Ellos—Mrs. Clemm, Virginia, algunas otras mujeres, ¡siempre mujeres!—sabrán de
> sus lágrimas, de su terror, de su necesidad de refugiarse en ellas, de ser mimado. . . .
> sólo consigo mismo condescendía a hablar. Por eso no le importaba que sus seres
> queridos no lo comprendieran. Le bastaba su cariño y su cuidado; no los necesitaba
> para la confidencia intelectual.(*OP*, pp. LIX-LX)

Indeed, while Poe was married to Virginia Clemm, both his needs for the
figure of the mother that sheltered and protected and for the figure of the
ethereal feminine presence that represented beauty, purity, and inspiration
were satisfied, the first in the figure of Mrs. Clemm, the second in Virginia.
Yet, the stories Poe conceived from the time when he first started thinking of
marrying Virginia ("Berenice") and throughout his married life with her until
soon after her death ("Morella," "Ligeia," "The Fall of the House of Usher,"
"The Oval Portrait," "The Oblong Box") display his deeper feelings regarding
his apparently "happy" domestic situation. In his stories, the ideal Feminine of
the poems is transformed into a fierce, overwhelming figure that threatens to
destroy and, in fact, destroys the hero. The ideal/terrible wives in Poe's tales
(all of whom possess traits that liken them to Virginia in one way or another)
are actually the victims of Poe's inner resentment against women for his need
of them and his humiliating inability to break away from them. His feminine

characters seem to combine Virginia's characteristics with Mrs. Clemm's, of whom one critic has observed, "her possessiveness had an animal ferocity."[8] However, the fact that Virginia and Mrs. Clemm were, in real life, two different persons, seems to have relegated the element of dread to the stories, keeping it apart from his own life experience. When Virginia died, Poe was left under the protection—and the threat—of the mother figure alone. It was at this time that he met Mrs. Whitman who, conveniently, possessed the attributes of both the mother and the maiden in herself. She was ten years older than he; yet, she was young-looking and, from all accounts, very attractive. She was also a literary woman who was capable of admiring Poe in the whole extent of his stature (unlike Virginia, who had only succumbed to a blind admiration for her older cousin "Eddie"). And she was rich, and "a personage," capable of advancing his literary aspirations. That Helen was, indeed, a sort of synthesis of Poe's dreams is apparent in his own letters to her:

> And now, in the most simple words at my command, let me paint to you the impression made upon me by your personal presence.—As you entered the room, pale, timid, hesitating, and evidently oppressed at heart; as your eyes rested appealingly, for one brief moment, upon mine, I felt, for the first time in my life, and tremblingly acknowledged, the existence of spiritual influences altogether out of the reach of reason. I saw that you were *Helen—my* Helen—the Helen of a thousand dreams—she whose visionary lips had so often lingered upon my own in the divine trance of passion—she whom the great Giver of all Good had preordained to be mine—mine only—if not now, alas! then at least thereafter, and *forever*, in the Heavens.—You spoke falteringly and seemed scarcely conscious of what you said. I heard no words—only the soft voice, more familiar to me than my own, and more melodious than the voice of the angels. Your hand rested within mine, and my whole soul shook with a tremulous ecstasy. And then but for very shame—but for the fear of grieving or oppressing you—I would have fallen at your feet in as pure—in as *real* a *worship* as was ever offered to Idol or to God. [Poe's italics][9]

Whether or not a great deal of the bombast in this letter can be traced to the common idiom in late nineteenth-century love letters, the words "you were *Helen—my* Helen—the Helen of a thousand dreams" indicate that Poe had indeed encountered, in real life and now an adult, a person that corresponded to the archetype he had long carried within himself.[10] His love for Helen is accompanied—however—by what seems to be his *dread* of Helen and his need to protect himself from the feelings that she aroused in him. He found that "protection" in his relationship to Mrs. Nancy Richmond ("Annie"), whom he addressed as "sister" and who seems to have occupied a place analogous to that which Virginia had left vacant when she died.[11]

In his account of Poe's relationship to Mrs. Whitman, Cortázar emphasizes the element of dread, implying that there was a direct relationship between the anxiety he felt facing his impending marriage to Helen and his attempted suicide by taking an overdose of laudanum in Westford, following a quarrel with Mrs. Whitman.[12] According to him, it was not dread of losing Helen, but that of *marrying* her (or Elmira Shelton, afterwards) that caused Poe's manic behavior throughout this incident, and finally brought about his death. Several critics have interpreted his dual relationship with Helen and "Annie" stating that it was Annie he really loved, but that he wished to marry Helen because she gave him a greater security.[13] Cortázar, however, believes that Poe felt a magical attraction for Helen that upset his being to such a degree that he sought to protect himself from it in the "sister" figure of Annie (*OP*, pp. XLVIII-XLIX). And truly the presence—and indeed, the whole "issue"—of Helen unleashed such a catastrophic anxiety neurosis in Poe that he gave himself to drink, knowing this would alienate Helen from him and thus end the mounting tension of their impending marriage. Poe never recovered after this unfortunate period; in a poem to Annie, he described himself as one who was finally free from the burden of life. His desire to die, expressed in his increasing escapes *via laudanum*, had started to gain control of his actions. From Cortázar's point of view, Poe's call to Reynolds with his last breath is to be interpreted as the delirious man's identification of the Death whose tightening grip he felt and the gigantic white figure at the end of *The Narrative of Arthur Gordon Pym* (*OP*, p. LII).

In his comments about Poe's works themselves, Cortázar points out the gulf that separates Poe's characters from real life. In Poe's stories, he observes, love is manifested as a feeling that, centering on the ideal form of the beloved, completely rejects normal sexuality:

> Esta inhumanidad de sus personajes ha de manifestarse además en un rasgo que acentúa su apartamiento de los cuadros ordinarios: me refiero a la falta de una sexualidad normal. No se trata de que los personajes no amen, pues con frecuencia su drama nace de la pasión amorosa. Pero esta pasión no es un amor dentro de la dimensión erótica común, sino que se sitúa en planos de angelismo o satanismo, asume los rasgos propios del sádico, el masoquista y el necrófilo, escamotea todo proceso natural y los sustituye por una pasión que el héroe *es el primero en no saber cómo calificar*—cuando no calla, como Usher, aterrado por el peso de su culpa o su obsesión. (*OP*, p. LXXXIV; his italics)

Cortázar proceeds to state that Poe's characters' ideal love for angelic creatures and satanic hatred for real ones is best exemplified in "The Fall of the House of Usher," "Berenice," "Morella," "Ligeia," "Eleonora," "The Oval Portrait," and "The Oblong Box." In the stories mentioned by Cortázar, we find two main thematic nuclei: first, the theme of incest, manifested in the hero's sexless love for a closely related young woman ("Eleonora," "Berenice," "The Fall of the House of Usher"); and second, the hero's diminution and dread of an imposing and threatening celestial wife whose death causes the psychic destruction of her husband ("Morella," "Ligeia," "The Oblong Box," "The Oval Portrait"). In both groups of stories, however, the figure of the

Feminine is not only presented in the description of the character itself but also in the *atmosphere* which surrounds it and which seems to act as a projection of it or, indeed, as a more powerful presence than the character itself. Thus we may state that, while the heroine acts as positive or negative anima, the engulfing atmosphere around her gives her a projection as Terrible Mother.

In Poe's prose, atmospheres themselves are perhaps more horrible than the very events that take place in them or than the characters who provoke these events. This is especially true in the stories Cortázar mentioned and in the tales of the sea. In "The Fall of the House of Usher," we read:

> I looked upon the scene before me—upon the mere house, and the simple landscape features of the domain—upon the bleak walls—upon the vacant eye-like windows—upon a few rank sedges—and upon a few white trunks of decayed trees—with utter depression of soul. . . . There was an iciness, a sinking, a sickening of the heart—an unredeemed dreariness of thought which no goading of the imagination could torture into aught of the sublime. . . .[14]

Since the soul of man is one with the universe ("The Colloquy of Monos and Una," *Eureka*), the sickness of a man's soul is projected onto his house, and onto the very landscape that surrounds it. In "Ligeia," similarly, the mental aberrations of the hero determine those of his surroundings. The bridal chamber where the hero leads the Lady Rowena is described as "an endless succession of ghastly forms" or "simple monstrosities" that provoke a "phantasmagoric effect," heightened by an artificial current of wind that gives a "hideous and uneasy animation to the whole."[15] The "soul" of the mysterious ship in "MS. Found in a Bottle," similarly, ends by invading the very being of the sailor who has chanced to fall on it, at the brink of the maelstrom:

> The ship and all in it were imbued with the spirit of Eld. The crew glide to and fro like the ghosts of buried centuries; their eyes have an eager and uneasy meaning; and when their fingers fall athwart my path in the wild glare of the battle-lanterns, I feel as I have never felt before, although I have been all my life a dealer in antiquities, and have imbibed the shadows of fallen columns at Balbec, and Tadmor, and Persepolis, until my very soul has become a ruin.[16]

For Poe, objects reflect the "soul" of their owner and have the property of transmitting their essence to those that come into contact with them. In *Pym*, the natives of Tsalal attempt to destroy the crew of the *Jane Guy* by burning the ship itself.

"Engulfing" is the single word that best expresses the main effect of Poe's seas, ships, and enclosed precincts; the feeling of being absorbed and annihilated provokes a reaction of unspoken horror in the hero and is transmitted to the reader.

In Neumann's study, the very themes singled out above are seen as basic symbols that represent the "terrible" aspect of the Magna Mater. Water acts as an important symbol in Poe's prose; yet, his are not the life-sustaining waters, but the putrid, stagnant waters that engulf Roderick Usher or that open into the frightful maelstrom devouring those who come within reach of its greedy embrace. Likewise, most of Poe's landscapes are not presented as the idyllic, sensuous gardens and bowers of Keats, but as the torture chamber, the crypt, the coffin, the hold of a mutinous ship—in short, as the devouring maw and the tomb. The predominance of this kind of symbolism indicates— according to Neumann's classification (*GM*, pp. 39-45)—the presence of a Terrible Mother constellation in the person in question. What the configuration implies is a weakness at the center of the personality whereby the death urge is far more powerful than the life instinct; the desire to remain perennially beside the protective figure of the mother brings with it a rejection of life and, thus, of growth and development. The arresting of a normal development, however, "twists" the very personality, bringing visions of confinement, stagnation, and putrefaction. The Mother—the towering figure from which the ego cannot break away—is then seen as having a threatening, overwhelming aspect that colors the very atmosphere around her. The theme of incest is also related to this constellation; love for the mother or the sister is the expression of a rejection of everything that lies "outside" the world of the child and its mother; the house that shelters brother and sister is identical with the Mother. Moreover, the death wish plays a central role in this constellation; the idea of breaking away from the Mother causes such an acute anxiety that the person wishes to abandon all struggle and return, through death, to the womb of the Earth Mother. Incest and death wish, then, are intimately related since they both display a desire to melt into the body of the Magna Mater and return to its all-embracing womb.

House symbolism as allusive to the confining character of the Terrible Mother plays a prominent role in Poe's tales, particularly in "The Fall of the House of Usher," and it is communicated to Cortázar's early stories. "The Fall of the House of Usher" is the last link in a thematic chain of stories that had started with "Berenice"; in them, Poe explored, in a fictional way, his own feelings towards his cousin Virginia, who served as the prototype for the heroines in them. These stories seem to have exerted a strong magnetism on Cortázar, who reflects their theme and atmosphere in a number of his own early stories.

In "The Fall of the House of Usher" and Cortázar's "Casa tomada" the theme of escape from the real world and confinement in a house that is seen as a projection of the protagonists' selves and as a protection against intrusions from the outside world[17] is reinforced by the theme of incest underlying the relationships of both brothers and sisters. In both stories, the house which locks in the heroes and their sisters, "freezing" them into an imaginarily pro-longed childhood, acts as a symbolic sheltering, isolating Magna Mater by itself. Incestuous relationships are hinted at in both stories: Roderick Usher and his twin sister Madeline are united by "sympathies of a scarcely intelligible nature"[18]; the hero in Cortázar's story and his sister Irene, likewise, share coughs, nightmares, and insomnia (*B*, p. 16). The theme of incest betrays, according to Jungian theory, a desire to return to the primordial, paradisiacal state of unconsciousness for which the womb is the universal symbol: "It [incest] symbolizes the union of the ego with the individual's own unconscious, the 'other side'—a blood relationship within the psyche."[19] In Poe's story, the decay of the physical house is symbolic of the degeneration of its tenants, who have brought themselves to the point of madness through their total exclusion of the outside world; the house, observes the narrator, had become identified with its occupants and their character:

> The Usher race, all time-honoured as it was, had put forth, at no period, any enduring branch. . . . it was this deficiency, perhaps, of collateral issue, and the consequent undeviating transmission, from sire to son, of the patrimony with the name, which had, at length, so identified the two as to merge the original title of the state *in the quaint and equivocal appellation of the 'House of Usher,'—an appellation which seemed to include, in the minds of the peasantry who used it, both the family and the family mansion.* [My italics][20]

In Cortázar's story, similarly, the house contains and represents the protagonists' past and childhood: "Nos gustaba la casa porque aparte de espaciosa y antigua . . . guardaba los recuerdos de nuestros bisabuelos, el abuelo paterno, nuestros padres y toda la infancia" (*B*, p. 9). The house, in Poe's story, is given a human presence and, with it, the power to intervene *actively* in the destinies of the brother and sister it shelters: "He [Usher] was enchained by certain superstititious impressions in regard to the dwelling which he tenanted, and whence, for many years, he had never ventured forth . . . an influence which some peculiarities in the mere form and substance of his family mansion, had, by dint of long sufferance, he said, obtained over his spirit. . . ."[21] Likewise, in Cortázar's story, the devouring and aggressive character of the house becomes explicit: "A veces llegamos a creer que era ella [the house] la que no nos dejó casarnos" (*B*, p. 9). The sinking of the House of Usher in the stagnant waters that surrounded it is paralleled, in Cortázar's story, by the expulsion of the brother and sister from the house. In the first, drowning is symbolic of the engulfment of the hero's consciousness by the Magna Mater; in the second, expulsion from the house (the Mother) is involuntary and dreaded and implies, as well, a loss of consciousness.

"La puerta condenada" also utilizes the house as a symbol of the womb or the mother; the hotel is described as "sombrío, tranquilo, casi desierto," and its atmosphere is characterized by "la falta de sol y aire" (*F*, p. 41); it resembles the Usher mansion, which allows "no disturbance from the breath of external air" and is only illuminated by "feeble gleams of encrimsoned light [which] made their way through the trellised panes, and served to render sufficiently distinct the more prominent objects around."[22] The atmosphere of the hotel suggests in itself the idea of "suppression" and anticipates the presence of the mother and child whom the protagonist hears behind the blocked door.

House symbolism is again present in "Carta a una señorita en París" and "Cefalea." In the first story, the protagonist temporarily occupies the apartment of a lady who has gone to Paris for the summer. From the very first sentence, the symbolic value of the house is made apparent: "Andrée, yo no quería venirme a vivir a su departamento de la calle Suipacha. No tanto por los conejitos, más bien porque me duele ingresar en un orden cerrado, construido ya hasta en las más finas mallas del aire" (B, p. 19). Further in the story, the identification between the house and its owner—the most salient symbolic detail in "The Fall of the House of Usher"—is reiterated:

> Me es amargo entrar en un ámbito donde alguien que vive bellamente lo ha dispuesto todo *como una reiteración visible de su alma.* . . . Ah, querida Andrée, qué difícil oponerse, aun aceptándolo con entera sumisión del propio ser, *al orden minucioso que una mujer instaura en su liviana residencia.* . . . Mover esa tacita altera el juego de relaciones de toda la casa, de cada objeto con otro, de *cada momento de su alma con el alma de la casa y su habitante lejana.* (B, pp. 19-20; my italics)

The protagonist's entrance into Andrée's world unleashes strange reactions in him; he begins to disgorge rabbits (a symbol of promiscuity and fertility). He is not cruel enough to kill the rabbits; but his fear of their doings in the house makes him become their slave. Every night he must feed them, clean the apartment of all traces of their presence and, later, repair the damages they occasion to the carpets, books, and furniture. Driven insane by his fear of the rabbits' destruction of the house, and by lack of sleep, he ends by throwing the rabbits off the balcony and jumping off after them.

Like "Carta a una señorita en París," "Cefalea" consists of an isolated madman's internal monologue which is highly reminiscent of those in Poe's stories. Like the hero in "Carta," the protagonist in this story externalizes his anxiety neurosis in the obsessive care of imaginary animals; the rabbits in "Carta" are paralleled, in this story, by the fantastic "mancuspias." The hero's mental state also provokes, as in "Usher," the identification of the house with the personality and, on a more understated level, with his dread of women. Usher's apprehension facing Madeline's presence and "Carta" 's protagonist's facing Andrée's house are paralleled in this story by the narrator's understated and equivocal feelings regarding a certain Leonor, who could be the protagonist's sister, wife, or mistress—we are not told which. The very ambiguousness of Leonor's presence, however, contributes to create the atmosphere of nightmare that is unleashed upon her disappearance. It is understood that Leonor elopes with Chango (a farmhand), leaving the protagonist alone in the house to handle by himself the daily ritual of the mancuspias' care and feeding. At the end of the story, the animals—as in "Carta"—break loose, wrecking the house and the farm. If the hero in "Carta" had been expelled by the house, the hero in this story is engulfed by it:

> El cráneo comprime el cerebro como un casco de acero—bien dicho. Algo viviente camina en círculo dentro de la cabeza. (*Entonces la casa es nuestra cabeza*, la sentimos rondada, *cada ventana es una oreja* contra el aullar de las mancuspias allá afuera. . . . No estamos inquietos, peor es afuera, si hay afuera. (*B*, pp. 89-90; my italics)

In Cortázar's stories, the animals play a role analogous to that of the lady Madeline in Poe's story; they are the ones who break loose and drive the hero to madness as they tear the house to pieces. They anticipate, thus, the role of "el perro" in *Rayuela* and *62*, even though, in these novels, the animal merely appears as a disembodied, ominous "presence." The symbolism of the house, however, appears to be connected with Poe's stories and the line "cada ventana es una oreja," specifically, is strongly reminiscent of the "vacant eye-like windows"[23] of the Usher mansion. Even though these stories—as all of Cortázar's earliest stories—also reflect a number of other influences from the masters of the horror story (as, for instance, the Maupassant of "The Horla," the Hoffmann of "The Sandman" and "Automata," and the Ambrose Bierce of "The Moonlit Road"), the use of house symbolism to convey the hero's obsession is distinctly traceable to Poe's influence.

The lingering effect of "The Fall of the House of Usher" on Cortázar can also be detected in "Relato con un fondo de agua," even though this story no longer centers on the symbol of the house, but on that of the island. The island in this story, however, displays the same qualities as the Usher mansion: isolation and decay. The mansion, as we might recall, had an "insular" quality about it, since it was totally surrounded by water. "Relato" is the dramatic monologue of an anonymous narrator who has retired to a primal world ("el Delta hubiera tenido que llamarse el Alfa," *F*, p. 139) in order to express his refusal to abandon the world of childhood:

> . . . lo terrible de ese momento de la juventud es que en una hora oscura y sin nombre todo deja de ser serio para ceder a la sucia máscara de seriedad que hay que ponerse en la cara, y yo ahora soy el doctor Fulano, y vos el ingeniero Mengano, bruscamente nos hemos quedado atrás, empezamos a vernos de otro modo aunque por un tiempo persistamos en los rituales, en los juegos comunes, en las cenas de camaradería que tiran sus últimos salvavidas en medio de la dispersión y el abandono, y todo es tan horriblemente natural, Mauricio, y a algunos les duele más que a otros, los hay como vos que van pasando por sus edades sin sentirlo. . . . (*F*, pp. 140-41)

Mauricio, the friend who visits the narrator in the Delta, plays an analogous role to that of the narrator in Poe's story; in both cases, the view of a "sane" character is juxtaposed to that of the "deranged" protagonist (in Cortázar's story, however, the narrator is the hero himself, while the "outsider" has a considerably less prominent role; Mauricio appears, in fact, merely as the shadow of Lucio, whose role parallels that of Madeline Usher). The heavy, silent, humid, decaying atmosphere of the island resembles that which surrounds the Usher mansion. The Delta is described as a "mundo remoto," "rancho medio podrido," whose atmosphere is characterized by an "aire pegajoso" and "barro amarillo." Even the vegetable and animal worlds gain a supernaturally threatening quality: as the protagonist walks with Lucio towards the scene of the dream, "un durazno podrido cayó con un golpe que tenía algo de bofetada" (F, p. 145), while the river "manoteaba solapado buscando donde agarrarse" (F, p. 142) and the frogs "ladraban como no ladran ni siquiera los perros" (F, p. 141).[24] There is an intimate connection between the atmosphere described above and that in "Usher," which is portrayed as

> an atmosphere which had no affinity with the air of heaven, but which had reeked up from the decayed trees, and the gray wall, and the silent tarn—a pestilent and mystic vapour, dull, sluggish, faintly discernible, and leaden-hued.[25]

In "Relato," the incestuous relationship between Usher and his sister is paralleled by an analogous situation: the homosexual relationship between the narrator and the disappeared Lucio.[26] In psychological terms, incest and homosexuality have analogous symbolic values, since both indicate a failure to grow beyond the initial narcissism of the child and imply a rejection of everything that is "different" or unknown.[27] Madeline, Usher's twin sister, and Lucio, the narrator's childhood friend, both confirm, through their relationship to the heroes, the narcissistic nature of these protagonists' loves.

In Poe's story, Roderick Usher, by killing his twin sister, who appears more as a double than as a sister, seems to kill his own soul; similarly, the narrator, by killing Lucio, kills his deeper self. Lucio had gone to the island, like himself, in search of "el pobre paraíso perdido que empecinadamente él volvía a buscar y yo me obstinaba en defenderle casi sin ganas" (F, p. 144). The parallelisms in the two stories are confirmed by the similarities in their final scenes. In Cortázar's story, the narrator is driven insane by a nightmare in which he sees Lucio, whom he had drowned, raise himself from the waters of the river and advance toward him, covered with filth and bitten by fish, determined to retaliate by drowning the protagonist:

> . . . entre todas esas manos de agua y juncos que resbalan en el barro y se deshacen en remolinos, hay unas manos que a esta hora se hincan en las raíces y no sueltan, algo trepa al muelle y viene aquí a buscarme. Todavía puedo dar vuelta a la moneda, todavía puedo matarlo de nuevo, pero se obstina y vuelve y alguna noche me llevará

con él. Me llevará, te digo, y el sueño cumplirá su imagen verdadera. Tendŕe que ir, la lengua de tierra y los cañaverales me verán pasar boca arriba, magnífico de luna, y el sueño estará al fin completo, Mauricio, el sueño estará al fin completo. (*F*, p. 146)

By juxtaposing this scene to that of Madeline Usher's ghostly return, we become aware of their similarities:

And now—to-night—Ethelred—ha! ha! the breaking of the hermit's door, and the death-cry of the dragon, and the clanguor of the shield—say, rather, the rending of her coffin, and the grating of the iron hinges of her prison, and her struggles within the coppered archway of the vault. . . . Oh whither shall I fly? Will she not be here anon? Is she not hurrying to upbraid me for my haste? Have I not heard her foot-step on the stair? Do I not distinguish that heavy and horrible beating of her heart? MADMAN! . . . MADMAN! I TELL YOU THAT SHE NOW STANDS WITHOUT THE DOOR![28]

Cortázar's story not only parallels the subject matter in Poe's, but the very language, tone, atmosphere, and dynamics in the story. Notice, for instance, the crescendo displayed in the two final scenes juxtaposed above, in which the heroes, collected up to that point, burst into insanity overcome with horror upon watching the return of the murdered "double."

However, the most startling connections between the two authors are to be found when comparing Cortázar's first two novels and Poe's *Narrative of Arthur Gordon Pym*. Poe's immediate motivation in writing *Pym* was apparently practical. Needing money, he remembered that his previous nautical account, "MS. Found in a Bottle" (1833), had been granted a prize because of its length and originality. Moreover, Poe had a "sixth sense" which enabled him to sort out the themes and situations most likely to captivate the public; he was very much aware of the then current fascination for nautical narratives and reports of Polar expeditions. As one Nathanael Ames—author of one among the numerous narratives of this kind—observed, at this time "every barber's clerk who crossed the ocean favored the public with his memoirs."[29] Like Melville some fifteen years later, Poe ·tried to fuse, in his narrative, heterogeneous materials drawn from the classics in the genre of the adventure story (Swift's *Gulliver's Travels*, Defoe's *Robinson Crusoe*, a new edition of which Poe had reviewed shortly before), the current fictional narratives of South Sea voyages (such as those written by Irving, Cooper, and Captain Marryat), and the actual accounts of contemporary expeditions to the South Pole that constantly appeared in newspapers and magazines. But most importantly, Poe subordinated all these influences to a central symbolic scheme derived from his own imagination and from his knowledge of mythology; through this scheme, he was to provide an outlet for the darkest visions of horror arising from the depths of his soul.

"MS. Found in a Bottle" had borrowed heavily from Jane Porter's review of *Sir Edward Seaward's Narrative, Or Symzonia: A Voyage of Discovery*, written by a certain "Captain Adam Seaborn" who was, in reality, Captain John Cleves Symmes.[30] In *Pym*, Poe borrowed even more from *Symzonia*; now, he seems to have been inspired, in his conception of Tsalal, by Symmes's description of a utopian civilization in the interior of the Earth. Symmes had developed and divulged the theory of the "holes at the Poles," claiming that there were corresponding openings in the North and South Poles, that the Earth was hollow and arranged in concentric spheres, that the waters of the oceans flowed through the Earth from one Pole to the other, and that access to the interior of the planet was possible through the "holes at the Poles."[31]

Another important source for *Pym* was the work of Jeremiah N. Reynolds—also a believer in the "holes at the Poles"—who in 1836 (the year before Poe started to work on *Pym*) had urged Congress to explore the South Seas. Poe had praised Reynolds' speech in the very issue of the *Southern Literary Messenger* that carried the first installment of *Pym*; years later, he was to call out to Reynolds with his dying breath. Other details were procured from Benjamin Morell's *Narrative of Four Voyages to the South Seas and Pacific, 1822-1831*; and still others from Poe's own childhood voyage to England aboard a "Flying Dutchman."[32]

Poe published the first chapters of *Pym* in the January and February 1837 issues of the *Messenger*. Several other chapters were composed soon after he moved to New York in February of that year. It was at this time that Poe reviewed J. T. Stephens' *Incidents of Travel in Egypt, Arabia and the Holy Land*, or *Arabia Petrea*, which seems to have had a great influence on the conception of the last chapters of *Pym*. It was in connection with the review of Stephens' work that he first sought scholarly information from Charles Anthon, the famous Professor of Classics at Columbia College and author of the *Classical Dictionary* that had synthesized the theories of the then revolutionary mythological syncretists.[33] Poe had no knowledge of Hebrew; however, his interest in the symbolism of Hebrew names and biblical symbolism is evident from the testimony of numerous passages in *Pinakidia*, a collection of notations which reflects Poe's constant interests just as much as *Marginalia* and *Fifty Suggestions*. Intrigued by a detail in Stephens' book, Poe wrote to Anthon, who replied with ample information about the point in question and cordially invited Poe to visit him;[34] this was the beginning of a friendship that was destined to play an important role in the genesis of *Pym*.

The review of *Arabia Petrea* appeared in *The New York Review* for October 1837; no credit was given to Anthon, however, and Poe subsequently used the material as his own. Bittner claims that Poe continued to rely on Anthon's erudition for matters concerning linguistics throughout the writing of *Pym*, [35] and I tend to agree with him, judging from the abundance of Hebrew words and names used to designate persons and places in the last section of *Pym*. I believe, moreover, that Anthon became Poe's consultant not only in matters of linguistics but of mythology as well. Poe's interest in the new theories about mythology, however, antedated his friendship with Anthon; *Pinakidia*—written in August 1836, one year before Poe moved to New York—abounds with references to matters often discussed in the works of the syncretists. Particularly, Poe seems to have held a special regard for the works of Jacob Bryant, whom he mentions at least five times on different occasions;[36] in one of the *Pinakidia* fragments he refers to him saying, "Bryant, whose authority we regard as superior to any" (XIV, 113). Killis Campbell observes that, in his Baltimore years, Poe possessed access to back numbers of British and American magazines, where themes fashionable among the intelligentsia were amply discussed;[37] more than likely, these magazines contained references to the theories of the mythological syncretists.

In any case, a number of symbolic allusions and names of deities in the last section of *Pym* seem to be directly related to George Stanley Faber's *On the Origin of Pagan Idolatry*, included in the list of sources for Anthon's Dictionary, as we shall see.

Cortázar seems to have been very sensitive to the elaborate, reiterative symbolic scheme created by Poe in *Pym*, as an analysis of Cortázar's first novel, *El examen*, will show.

In both *El examen* and *Pym*, the narrative thread connects a number of episodes by which the heroes are meant to be "initiated" into full manhood after a prolonged adolescence: Pym has to leave behind his sheltered existence as a well-to-do heir of a Nantucket family; Juan and Clara are to take "the exam" with which their student days will be over, and must afterwards leave "the city," which develops an almost anthropomorphic quality as the novel progresses. Both novels, moreover, present a symbolic *return to the origins*, in the historical as well as the psychological sense. Pym descends to the south and encounters the "black" primitive world of Tsalal where natives, like children, mentally belong to the preconceptual world of ritual. But the voyage to the south is also a voyage inwards, and the final descent to the cave of the White Figure is both an encounter with the primal deity or Magna Mater and with the psychological dread of annihilation she embodies. Similarly, Cortázar's novel presents a voyage in time. In *El examen* there is no nautical voyage to the south—since the characters *are* already in the south, in Río de la Plata—but there is a destruction, a rotting away analogous to the stage in Pym's voyage that precedes his entrance into Tsalal, and once the physical manifestations of "civilization" (the sidewalks, libraries, buildings, etc.) have been stripped away, a number of rituals take place in the streets of Buenos Aires as men dressed in black chant litanies around a *white figure* simply identified as "Ella."

According to Poe's theory of effect, every element must combine in order to produce the preconceived reaction the author expects from the reader. No detail is superfluous or haphazardly chosen in *Pym*; all elements in the narrative are meant to prepare for the climax, the awesome appearance of the White Figure. We have seen that the ship, according to Faber's theories, was one of the symbols that alluded to the Magna Mater; but the ship that carries Pym south into the world of Tsalal and Tsalemon, the *Jane Guy* from Liverpool, has, moreover, a woman's name. The climax is anticipated by the white animals with red fangs and claws that Pym's companions find in Tsalal. These creatures excite a feeling of panic among the natives, who retreat in horror amidst shouts of "Tekeli-li" and "Anamoo-moo" whenever they catch a glimpse of the animals' white fur. Evidently, their horror arises from the association of the white fur with the White Figure. Another seemingly insignificant incident gains unsuspected importance as we proceed in the narrative. In the episode when the natives first board the *Jane Guy*, we are told that the cook, carelessly chopping wood on deck, lets the hatchet slip and drives it into the *Jane*'s side:

> The chief immediately ran up, and pushing the cook on one side rather roughly, commenced a half-whine, half-howl, strongly indicative of sympathy in what he considered the sufferings of the schooner, patting and smoothing the gash with his hand, and washing it from a bucket of seawater which stood by.[38] (*Pym*, p. 143)

What appears as merely an amusing episode at first gains relief when we later associate the "personification" of the *Jane* with the overall personification of Tsalal, whose rivers appear like veins in one enormous body, and their waters, like blood:

> Upon collecting a basinful, and allowing it to settle thoroughly, we perceived that the whole mass of liquid was made up of a number of distinct veins, each of a distinct hue; that these veins did not conmingle; and that their cohesion was perfect in regard to their own particles among themselves and imperfect in regard to neighboring veins. . . . The phenomenon of this water formed the first definite link in that vast chain of apparent miracles with which I was destined to be at length encircled. (*Pym*, pp. 146-47)

Poe's passion for cryptography is too well known to assume that the names of the region, the natives, and the White Figure were casually chosen. Sidney Kaplan has observed that "Tsalal" is actually the Hebrew word for "to be dark"; its chief is Too-Wit, the Hebrew for "to be dirty"; the chief of the archipelago is Tsalemon, the Hebrew for "shady."[39] Poe knew no Hebrew; the names were probably derived from one of the many comparative linguistic studies[40] that had appeared in the wake of the renewed interest in myth, anthropology, and linguistics, or from Anthon himself.[41] Most of these studies followed the comparative and syncretic method displayed in Bryant's *Mythology*, especially in the section on "Radicals," where he stated that common names of places (Kir, Air, Kol, Cala, Ai, Ain) that often recurred in Babylonia and Egypt constituted "so many elements, whence most names in ancient mythology have been compounded, and into which they are attended, will, at all times, plainly point out, and warrant the etymology."[42]

In Faber's treatise we read:

> All the Goddesses of Paganism will be found ultimately to melt together into a single person, who is at once acknowledged to be the great mother and the earth: yet that person is declared to have assumed the form of a ship when the mighty waters of the vast deep universally prevailed, to have peculiarly presided over navigation, to have sprung from the sea and yet to have been born from that sacred mountain whence flowed the holy rivers of Paradise, to have contained within her womb all those hero-gods who are literally said to have each sailed in an ark, or to have had a ship as her special representative.[43]

Faber's essay proceeds to consider legendary instances of the hero's exposure to an ark, his enclosure inside it, its identification with the miraculous ship in myth, legend, and folklore, and its association with the extraordinary voyage. There seems to be a particularly revealing relationship between the descent in the final chapters of *Pym* and the hero's encounter of a gigantic white figure emerging from a crevice in a rock and Faber's discussion of the symbols that allude to the Magna Mater:

> We shall equally find in romance the sacred lake, the fairy or female divinity presiding over it, the wonderful cavern, the oracular tomb or imprisonment, the sleeping giant, and the upright figure eternally seated upon a large stone like the Memnon and other colossal statues of Egypt.[44]

I believe that, while Poe was naturally predisposed—because of his peculiar psychic configuration, shaped by the tragic deaths of the women he had loved as a child and adolescent—to a number of symbols that identified women with death, the theories of the syncretists with which he became acquainted, especially through Anthon, helped refine and develop the symbols around which he was to build the stories of the sea and *Pym*. Similarly, I believe that Cortázar's constant interest in the works of Poe and the two years he spent in close scrutiny of Poe's texts while carrying out his translation favored his absorption of Poe's techniques in the presentation of an archetype Cortázar himself was extremely sensitive to.

Both "Anamoo-moo" and "Tekeli-li" are compounded with one or more of those basic radicals singled out by Bryant. But "Ana," especially, recurs in the mythologies of Asia Minor to designate the Mother Goddesses. Poe was as sensitive to the name "Anna" as he was to that of "Helen"; he called Mrs. Nancy Richmond "Annie" and the poem where he celebrated his love for Virginia Clemm was called "Annabel Lee." As Robert Graves observes in *The White Goddess*, "if one needs a single, simple, inclusive name for the Great Goddess, Anna is the best choice."[45] Poe, evidently, had not read Graves; but he had read Anthon's Dictionary, whose entries for "Ana" and "Anna" identify this name with the primal Magna Mater.[46] The particle "moo-moo" recalls both the child's babble for "mother" and the word "moon," also an attribute of "Anna Perenna." "Tekeli-li," on the other hand, resembles the name of the Sumerian goddess Belili[47]—a sister to Anna Perenna—and the Babylonian moon goddess, Ishtar Kilili, or simply Kilili. Ishtar was a twofold goddess, the creator and the destroyer, and conforms to the containing and absorbing character of the White Figure. Kilili means "she who leans out," and she was presented in temples peering from a window or a crevice;[48] the White Figure, likewise, appears within a crevice, the cataract ("And now we rushed into the embraces of the cataract, where a chasm threw itself open to receive us. But there arose in our pathway a shrouded human figure, very far larger in its proportions than any dweller among men," *Pym*, p. 185). The "Te" would appear as a remnant of "Ishtar" or as a corruption of "Thea" or "Dea."[49]

Just as he had been fascinated—at about this time—by Keats's mythological projections of the Feminine in *Lamia* and "La Belle Dame," so Cortázar was deeply impressed by Poe's depiction of the Feminine not only in the form of the gigantic, indefinite White Figure at the end of the narrative but also in the form of the ship, the sea, the rivers and the caverns themselves, and, on a larger scale, as the whole realm of Tsalal and Tsalemon—the realm of "darkness"—into which Pym and Peters venture, as if they journeyed, indeed, inside the womb of the Great Mother. In *El examen* the city itself becomes a symbol of the forces that fetter and confine the hero, Andrés Fava, and later, as it rots, of devouring and all-embracing Death. It is after the river retires and the putrefaction spreads that "Ella," and later the Eighty Women, make their triumphal entrance. "Ella" is as inseparable from "the city" as the White Figure was from Tsalal.

Poe had resorted to the erudition and cultural "fads" of his times to elaborate "conceits" for the names in his narrative; Cortázar, rather than adopting the names utilized by Poe, turned to names that would be relevant to the readers of *his own* times, while conveying, like Poe's, the numinosity of the archetypal Feminine in his novel. Poe had recurred to Anthon's Dictionary and the treatises by Bryant and perhaps Faber; Cortázar, on the other hand, apparently consulted C. G. Jung's *The Archetypes and the Collective Unconscious*, a widely read and discussed work at that time. In this work, Jung includes at least six mentions of H. Rider Haggard's novel *She* ("Ella"), a novel which he believes presents the anima concept and "the symbolic context in which the archetype is usually embedded"[50] better than any other literary work. "She"—Jung states—typifies the archetype's characteristic ambivalence: she is both young and old, good and bad, and moreover, she has " 'occult' connections with 'mysteries,' with the world of darkness in general. . . . Whenever she emerges with some degree of clarity, she always has a peculiar relationship to *time*: as a rule she is more or less immortal, because outside of time."[51] Cortázar apparently established a connection in his mind between the two novels (*She* presents a number of similarities with *Pym*, since it deals, as well, with a voyage to uncharted southern regions, an encounter with an isolated primitive people who dread the authority of a mysterious female dressed in white) and retained the atmosphere of Poe's narrative while presenting the personified Magna Mater under a form more reminiscent of Haggard's.[52]

Just as Pym had been associated with two "doubles"—the frail Augustus, who dies aboard the drifting hulk, and the strong hybrid Peters, who accompanies Pym in the last stage of his journey—Andrés Fava is associated with the mysterious Abel, a character who is alluded to throughout the novel, but who appears only at the very end. Abel had been in love with Clara and now seems to present a vague threat to Juan, who married her, and a more serious one to Andrés, who loves her in secret. Andrés is also associated with a nameless young man who dies in front of Andrés' eyes halfway through the novel. As the rites in the city multiply, Andrés feels threatened; his dread mounts when he observes a contingent of Eighty Women who seem to take control of the city. Further, he observes a group of children bathing in a enormous tin tub. The bath—or any other form of immersion in water—is traditionally associated in alchemical and occult symbolism with rebirth.[53] The presence of *children* bathing seems to emphasize the symbolic value of this action; however, Andrés does not respond positively to them. Instead, they seem to augment his fears. Both the Eighty Women and the children are regarded as heralds of catastrophe by Andrés, just as the veined waters of Tsalal had appeared to Pym as a prophecy of his doom.[54] After Andrés observes the children bathing in the tub, he witnesses the death of an unknown young man. He is utterly shaken at the death of this young man whom he seems to regard as a projection of his own younger self. He seems to be unable to erase the picture of the "victim"—as he calls the deceased—from his mind; the final section of the novel is occupied with Andrés' long internal monologue about the horrors of death and putre-faction of the flesh. Finally, he helps Juan and Clara escape the decaying city, but he stays in order to face his double, Abel.

The ending of *El examen* is as irregular as that of *Pym*. In *El examen*, Andrés dies at the hands of Abel; yet, when I asked Cortázar for an explana-tion of the ending, he said that after Andrés had helped Juan and Clara to escape, he no longer wanted to live: ". . . cuando Andrés alza la pistola, no es a Abel a quien mata. Se mata a sí mismo y, naturalmente, Abel es destruido a la vez, puesto que no tenía una realidad independiente."[55] There seems to be a contradiction between the fear of death evinced in Andrés' long monologue after the death of his first double and the suicide through the murder of the second double implied at the end of the novel. Death wish enacted in the murder of the double is a recurring theme in Poe's stories ("The Cask of Amontillado," "The Tell-Tale Heart," "The Black Cat," etc.). It seems that Cortázar's thanatophobia and Poe's necrophilia spring from the same source: the desire to escape the fear of death and dissolution by a voluntary return to the womb of the Magna Mater. In his study of the theme of the double, Otto Rank interprets thanatophobia as the narcissistic wish to remain forever young and, thus, forever sheltered by the mother, free from the exigencies of life and from the ravages of time. Rank observes that, for the writers obsessed with the idea of death, it is not death itself, but the *expectation of death* which seems unbearable. The thought of the approaching dissolution of the self and the flesh "torments these unfortunates with the conscious idea of their eternal, eternal inability to return, an idea from which release is only possible in death. Thus we have the strange paradox of the suicide who voluntarily seeks death in order to free himself from the intolerable thanatophobia."[56] Both Pym and Andrés, having witnessed the horrors of death and decomposition in Augustus and the nameless young man—their respective doubles—retreat in horror of the organic life and strive to return to the sheltered world of the mother which, paradoxically, can only be reached through death. Pym's *desire to fall*—manifested in the episode when he and Peters enter the mysterious cavern with inscribed walls—is the unconquerable force that impels him to continue the descent in the last section of the novel. Likewise, it is Andrés' desire to die and avoid the mutations his self would have to undergo in life that makes him remain in the decaying city after he has helped Juan and Clara to escape. Both novels end at the point at which the heroes reach the final confrontation with the Mother/Death. No attempts are made to return the heroes to the diurnal world. As far as the authors are concerned, the heroes have reached their destination.

The influence of *Pym* is even more patent in Cortázar's next novel, *Los premios*. The intervening years have seen Cortázar's translations of Poe's prose works; and the effect of Cortázar's close analysis of Poe's techniques can be felt more than in his previous works. Cortázar seems to have learned an important lesson from Poe: that of communicating the whole depth of horror by *suggesting*, rather than stating. *El examen*'s long monologues about death and putrefaction are now replaced by a number of symbols and situations that suggest a descent unto death without portraying it directly. The mysterious and engulfing quality of the sea surrounding the *Malcolm* conveys the whole depth of mystic horror in the manner of Rimbaud's "Le Bateau ivre," also inspired by *Pym*, "MS. Found in a Bottle," and "A Descent into the Maelström." Moreover, the ship moves *towards the south*, as in Poe's narrative. The south, since it is positioned "below" or "under," refers not only to the unconscious but also to the Feminine, to the Mother (*GM*, pp. 39-54). The atmosphere of darkness, confinement, oppression, and silence suggests a mystical quest from the very beginning and recalls the novel's most important models: Coleridge's "Rime of the Ancient Mariner," Conrad's "The Secret Sharer," Rimbaud's "Le Bateau ivre," and, most importantly, *The Narrative of Arthur Gordon Pym*. Direct references to these works can be found throughout the novel. At one point:

Persio siente como un espanto que sube peldaño a peldaño, visiones de barcas fatales sin timonel corren por su memoria, lecturas recientes lo proveen de visiones donde la siniestra región del noroeste (y Tuculca con un caduceo verde en la mano, amenazante) se mezclan con Arthur Gordon Pym y la barca de Erik en el lago subterráneo de la Opera, vaya mescolanza. (*P*, p. 101)

The tension latent in the atmosphere is suddenly concentrated on the prohibition against descending to the stern of the ship. The prohibition is not stated in so many words, and that makes it even more humiliating. But after a while we realize that the stern itself hides nothing in particular—a fact that is confirmed at the end of the novel—but it is symbolic of each character's darkest fears. As Raúl states early in the novel, "no creo que haya ninguna tomadura de pelo sino que somos víctimas de una especie de estafa. Nada que se parezca a las estafas comunes, por supuesto; algo más . . . metafísico . . ." (*P*, p. 150).

In *Pym*, the stern of the *Grampus* had acted as an initiatic cave where the hero underwent a symbolic death as a timid adolescent and a rebirth as the bolder man who helped Dirk Peters overcome the mutineers. The initiatic character of the stern in *Los premios* combines with the symbolic labyrinthine structure of the corridors leading to it; both together give each character's inner confrontation a quality of primitive ritual of death and rebirth, identifying, as in *El examen*, the psychological with the historical search for the origins.

According to Neumann, the labyrinth appears among the primitives' rites of passage as the symbol of the Terrible Mother (*GM*, pp. 62-63).[57] It certainly appears as such for Medrano, for whom it becomes symbolic of his labyrinthine relationships to women. Medrano joins the group in the *Malcolm* after abandoning his mistress Bettina without any particular reason; he admits there is something especially sadistic about his behavior, but still cannot understand the motivations for his action. The vague feeling of remorse at the beginning of the novel gradually increases until Medrano realizes he is faced with a problem on whose solution depends his very being: "Absurdo que la popa y Bettina fueran en ese momento un poco la misma cosa. . . . La popa y Bettina, era realmente estúpido que todo eso fuera ahora un punto doloroso en la boca del estómago" (*P*, p. 197). When Medrano meets Claudia, strange reactions are unleashed within him; for the first time, he becomes aware of the emptiness of his former existence and of his need for greater "human ties": "la mayor de sus culpas podía haber sido una libertad fundada en una falsa higiene de vida, un deseo egoísta de disponer de sí mismo en cada instante de un día reiteradamente único, sin lastres de ayer y de mañana. Visto con esa óptica, todo lo que llevaba andado se le aparecía de pronto como un fracaso absoluto" (*P*, p. 322). According to Saúl Sosnowski,[58] Medrano realizes, by meeting Claudia, that he had lived up to that moment according to inauthentic laws. Sosnowski specifies that Medrano wants Claudia *and* Jorge in his life. Certainly, it is not Claudia alone, but Claudia *as mother*, as the mother of a specially gifted child, that has a peculiar appeal for Medrano. Indeed, the close relationship between them is established the moment he recognizes her primarily *as a mother*:

> Sonrió al precisar el punto exacto—lo sentía así, estaba perfectamente seguro—en que ambos habían abandonado el peldaño ordinario para descender, como tomados de la mano, hacia un nivel diferente. . . . Había ocurrido en el momento preciso en que él—tan poco antes, realmente tan poco antes—le había dicho: "Madre de Jorge, el leoncito . . ." (*P*, p. 231)

Further on, just before Medrano's dreamlike vision, he repeats:

> Pero ¿por qué tenía que ser Claudia quien le abriera de golpe las puertas del tiempo, lo expulsara desnudo en el tiempo que empezaba a azotarlo obligándolo a fumar cigarrillo tras cigarrillo, morderse los labios y desear que de una manera u otra el puzzle acabara por recomponerse, que sus manos inciertas, novicias en esos juegos, buscaran tanteando los pedazos rojos, azules y grises, extrajeran del desorden un perfil de mujer, un gato ovillado junto al fuego, un fondo de viejos árboles de fábula? (*P*, p. 323)

The images used in connection with Claudia indicate childbirth: she had "expelled him naked into the world," she had "suddenly opened to him the gates of time." Moreover, he says he needed Claudia's help to recompose the "puzzle." What does the scene in the puzzle (a woman's profile, a cat by the fire, old trees in the background) represent? Perhaps a scene in the character's childhood? We are never told. But right after this realization on Medrano's part, the dream sequence takes place.

In Medrano's reverie, Bettina pushes aside the drapes that hid her and walks toward the center of the room, her face still concealed by her hair. Medrano is overcome with horror and cannot escape. Then Bettina uncovers her face, and Medrano feels "un estallido de claridad y consumación, la amenaza por fin concretada y resuelta, el fin de todo, la presencia absoluta del horror en esa hora y ese sitio . . ." (*P*, p. 325). He is seized by a mounting unexplained dread of Bettina and tries to escape the sight of her weeping, accusing face, to no avail. Later, Medrano tries to explain the dream by saying it was himself, his own nature, that was revealed in it.

Like the White Figure at the end of *Pym*, Bettina becomes a synthesis and symbol of Woman which has acquired a monstrous and supernatural dimension for the hero: Bettina becomes "una Bettina monstruosa frente a la cual la mujer que había sido su amante se deshacía como él mismo se sentía deshacer mientras poco a poco retrocedía hasta la puerta . . ."; she has grown to a supernatural stature and her face is no longer that of a particular woman, but ". . . el revés de Bettina, una máscara donde un sufrimiento inhumano, *una concentración de todo el sufrimiento del mundo* sustituía y pisoteaba la triviali-dad de una cara . . ." (*P*, pp. 325-26; my italics). Like Pym, Medrano has finally achieved a "descent" to his inner self, just as Pym had descended "into the embraces of the cataract," and found the figure of a woman that was more than a woman ("la cara de Bettina era un mundo infinito") and at whose sight he is seized with horror, feeling "un estallido de claridad y consumación . . . la presencia absoluta del horror en esa hora y ese sitio . . ." (*P*, p. 325). The "Bettina monstruosa" plays an analogous role to that of the "shrouded human figure, very far larger in its proportions than any dweller among men" that Pym encounters at the end of his voyage and whose meeting, apparently, he does not survive. The last words in the appendix attached to *Pym*—where Poe once again insists on the association of the shout of "Tekeli-li" and whiteness (Kilili is the "White Goddess")—allude to the meaning of the hieroglyphs on the walls of the cavern, which announce the figure's supernatural revenge: "I HAVE GRAVEN IT WITHIN THE HILLS, AND MY VENGEANCE UPON THE DUST WITHIN THE ROCK" (*Pym*, p. 188). Bettina, likewise, is metamorphosed into the image of the avenging Terrible Mother, making Medrano feel "*el momento más atroz de una tortura* pero sin dolor físico, *la esencia de la tortura* sin el retorcimiento de la carne y los nervios" (*P*, p. 325; my italics). Pym does not survive the confrontation with the figure; Medrano does, briefly, but only physically. Psychologically, Bettina has destroyed him by actually impeding all his prospects of a more meaningful life with Claudia: all that remains in him is "una sensación de que *cada elemento de su vida, de su cuerpo, de su pasado y su presente eran falsos,* y que la falsedad estaba ahí al alcance de la mano . . ." (*P*, p. 326; my italics). In both nightmarish visions, a Terrible Mother claims back unto herself the life that had attempted to break away from her all-powerful embrace.

Medrano's almost obsessive longing for the "Good Mother" figure of Claudia is reversed by his confrontation with the Terrible Mother figure of Bettina; the latter stands for all the women Medrano has abandoned, including, thus, *his mother.* With vindictive ferocity, she returns to impede the consummation of Medrano's love for Claudia. The underlying theme of the ghostly apparition who usurps her rival's place in this episode seems to have provoked its unconscious—or perhaps conscious—identification in Cortázar's mind with the scene of Ligeia's return. In "Ligeia," the hero's deceased wife returns and occupies, for a spell, the body of her rival, the hero's new wife, the Lady Rowena. A juxtaposition of specific passages describing Ligeia's return and Bettina's apparition will illustrate the striking parallels between them. In Cortázar's novel we read:

Era casi natural, casi necesario que Bettina descorriera uno de los raídos cortinados y avanzara hacia él como resbalando sobre la mugrienta alfombra, se parara a menos de un metro y alzara poco a poco la cara completamente tapada por el pelo rubio. La sensación de amenaza se disolvía, viraba a otra cosa sin que él supiera todavía qué era esa otra cosa aun peor que iba a suceder. . . . Medrano hubiera querido retroceder, sentir por lo menos la espalda pegada a la puerta, pero flotaba en un aire pastoso del que tenía que extraer cada bocanada con un esfuerzo del pecho, de todo el cuerpo. . . . (P, p. 324)

And in "Ligeia":

> . . . arising from the bed, tottering, with feeble steps, with closed eyes, and with the manner of one bewildered in a dream, the thing that was enshrouded advanced boldly and palpably into the middle of the apartment. I trembled not—I stirred not—for a crowd of unutterable fancies connected with the air, the stature, the demeanor of the figure, rushing hurriedly through my brain, had paralyzed—had chilled me into stone. I stirred not—but gazed upon the apparition. There was a mad disorder in my thoughts—a tumult unappeasable.[59]

Both figures appear in a dark, curtained room (Ligeia arises from the bed; Bettina emerges from behind the curtains) and walk towards the middle of the room, their faces concealed. The heroes attempt to evade the "visions," but horror freezes them into immobility while their anticipation of the apparitions' next move threatens to overturn their minds. Further parallels are to be found in both figures' sudden unveiling of their faces and the terrifying expression with which they fix their eyes on the heroes' faces:

Cortázar:

> Cuando sacudió la cabeza y todo el pelo saltó hacia atrás, derramándose sobre las orejas y los hombros, su rostro estaba tan cerca del suyo que con sólo inclinarse hubiera podido mojar sus labios en las lágrimas que lo empapaban. . . . desorbitados los ojos . . . interrogaban a Medrano, y cada pestaña, cada pelo de las cejas parecía aislarse, dejarse ver por sí mismo y por separado, la cara de Bettina era un mundo infinito, fijo y convulso a la vez delante de sus ojos que no podían evadirla. (P, p. 324)

Poe:

> she let fall from her head, unloosened, the ghastly cerements which had confined it, and there streamed forth, into the rushing atmosphere of the chamber, huge masses of long and disheveled hair; *it was blacker than the raven wings of midnight!* And now slowly opened *the eyes* of the figure which stood before me. "Here then, at least," I shrieked aloud, "can I never—can I never be mistaken—these are the full, and the black and the wild eyes—of my lost love—of the lady—of the LADY LIGEIA." [Poe's italics][60]

Both heroes are unable to proceed on their journeys after their confrontations with the archetypal Terrible Mother. Poe concludes his narrative observing that the "few remaining chapters" of the narrative "have been irrecoverably lost." Cortázar, equally at a loss regarding the future course his hero will follow, decides to kill him. Indeed, it seems that Medrano deliberately seeks

death in order to avoid the problems arising from a life with Claudia and the
necessary development of his own character. She herself denounces his action
as a cowardice, as a treason:

> pensó que él la había necesitado y que era una traición y una cobardía marcharse
> así, abandonarse a sí mismo a la hora del encuentro. . . . Se iba como si tuviera
> miedo, elegía la más vertiginosa de las fugas, la de la inmovilidad irremediable, la
> del silencio hipócrita. . . . Todo eso hubiera podido cesar si él no estuviese ahí con
> las pruebas del robo y del abandono, *si no se hubiera hecho matar como un tonto
> para no llegar a vivir de verdad en ella* y hacerla vivir con su propia vida. (*P*,
> pp. 393-94; my italics)

But his actions can be interpreted—as Horacio Oliveira's suicide or madness
at the end of *Rayuela*, which it anticipates—as his refusal to betray the world
of childhood (and thus, of the mother) by becoming a man and breaking away
from the Magna Mater's embrace. In a supreme rejection of everything that
lies outside and beyond the world of the child and the adolescent, the hero
expresses his faithfulness to the Magna Mater by surrendering to the overpowering presence of the Terrible Mother as Death.

PART II

Rites and Mysteries

3

The Individual Quest

Whether the hero be ridiculous or sublime, Greek or barbarian, gentile or Jew, his journey varies little in essential plan. Popular tales represent the heroic action as physical; the higher religions show the deed to be moral; nevertheless, there will be found astonishingly little variation in the morphology of the adventure, the character roles involved, the victories gained. If one or another of the basic elements of the archetypal pattern is omitted from a given fairy tale, legend, ritual or myth, it is bound to be somehow or other implied—and the omission itself can speak volumes for the history and pathology of the example. . . .

Joseph Campbell
The Hero With a Thousand Faces

After the work of the psychoanalysts in the past few decades, no one can seriously doubt the profound psychological significance of mythological symbolism. Sigmund Freud, Carl Gustav Jung, Otto Rank, Géza Róheim, Erich Neumann, and others have developed a vastly documented body of dream and myth interpretation, and with their discovery that the patterns and logic of fairy tales and myth correspond to those of dreams, it has been shown that myths are of the nature of dreams, and that dreams can be studied as symptomatic of the dynamics of the psyche. This assertion becomes extremely relevant when embarking upon a study of certain works by Keats, Poe, and Cortázar in which mythological symbolism is, indeed, characterized by a process of reelaboration whereby a number of "given" mythic situations are transformed and reshaped by the peculiar nightmares or obsessions of the author in question. The concatenation of a number of episodes into a "ritualistic" structure that denotes the hero's spiritual "progression" plays a central role in the development of a number of Keats's, Poe's, and Cortázar's narrative schemes.

Among the primitives, tribal ceremonies of birth, initiation, marriage, burial, installation, and so forth, serve to relate the individual's own experience to larger, impersonal, archetypal forms. Through ritual, a social group becomes aware of a transcending element behind and beyond its daily toils: individuals may pass, but the eternal forms remain. Hence, ritual leads the individual to the realization that he is not "alone" or "different" when he undergoes an experience that is new or unknown to him; but he is enhanced, supported, and magnified through his identification with the archetypal superindividual. Through ritual, he becomes Everyman. If personal rites of passage establish a link between the individual and his specific social group, the seasonal festivals and mysteries link man, as a race, with the processes that direct the eternal transmutations in nature, presenting humanity as an integral part of a macrocosmos. But there is another kind of rite in addition to the popular cult of social integration or to the natural mysteries: that of the Hellenistic mystery initiations, medieval mysticism, and the ancient philosophies of the East. In them, the aim of the ritual is to *separate* the individual from the temporary concerns of his particular social group and allow him to concentrate on the core of human existence, on the search for his identity and for his place and meaning within the macrocosmos.

For the ancients all meaning was to be found in the life of the group, and the mysteries and perils lay without; the rites of passage, thus, were mainly an expression of the individual's ties with a specific group. For contemporary man the world outside is no longer a mystery (or, in any case, it is not the main object of his philosophical speculations), and the ties and rituals of the group have lost their meaning and their ability to bind. After the Romantic movement, the motif of the spiritual or individual quest gained an overwhelming ascendance over the motif of the collective quest. The Romantics, with their interest in the new mythologies that were being discovered and interpreted (Nordic, Persian, Egyptian, Hindu mythologies had been largely unknown in Europe until 1790, approximately), encountered initiatory patterns that had lost their ritual reality, and transmuted these patterns into literary motifs that now delivered their message on a different plane of experience, by addressing themselves to the imagination. In the hands of the Romantics, the quest became, more than ever before, a quest for the soul, for the identity, for man's place in an increasingly alien universe.

The archetypal quest pattern formed by the adventures of the mythological hero is an amplification of the formula represented in rites of passage: SEPARATION–INITIATION–RETURN. Joseph Campbell terms this basic pattern "the nuclear unit of the monomyth": "A hero ventures forth from the world of common day into a region of supernatural wonder: fabulous forces are there encountered and a decisive victory is won: the hero comes back from this mysterious adventure with the power to bestow boons on his fellow man."[1] Schema III will serve to illustrate the nuclear unit or basic structure of the quest.

Yet even if this basic pattern is to be discovered behind the diverse forms in which the adventures of the hero become manifest, it is not to be confused with the *personally modified* symbolic figures that appear in the nightmares

call to adventure

helper

elixir

threshold crossing
brother-battle
dragon-battle
dismemberment
crucifixion
abduction
night-sea journey
wonder journey
whale's belly

threshold of adventure

return
resurrection
rescue
threshold struggle

tests

flight

helpers

1. sacred marriage
2. father atonement
3. apotheosis
4. elixir theft

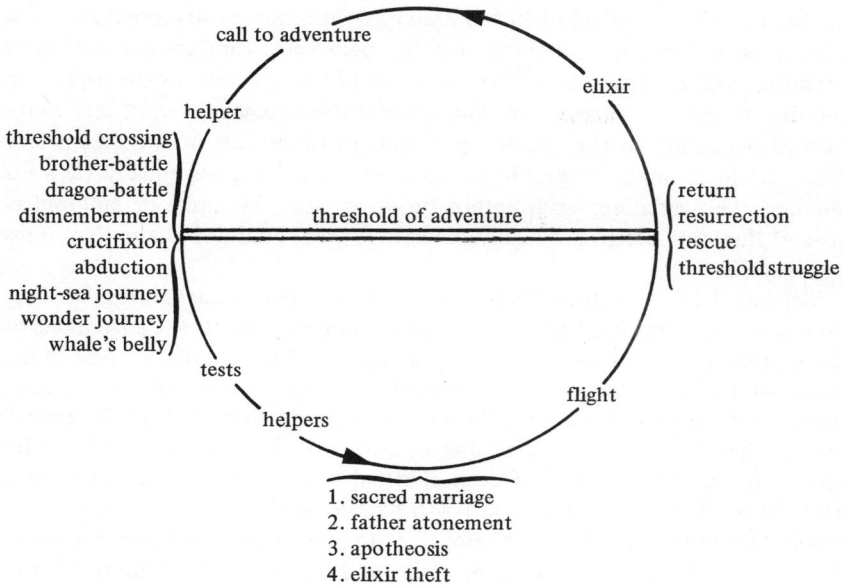

SCHEMA III—Structure of the Monomyth.
Joseph Campbell, *The Hero With a Thousand Faces*, Bollingen Series XVII. Copyright 1949 by Princeton University Press. Copyright © renewed 1976 by Princeton University Press. Schema on p. 245. Reproduced by permission.

"The mythological hero, setting forth from his commonday hut or castle, is lured, carried away, or else voluntarily proceeds, to the threshold of adventure. There he encounters a shadow presence that guards the passage. The hero may defeat or conciliate this power and go alive into the kingdom of the dark (brother-battle, dragon-battle; offering, charm), or be slain by the opponent and descend in death (dismemberment, crucifixion). Beyond the threshold, then, the hero journeys through a world of unfamiliar yet strangely intimate forces, some of which severely threaten him (tests), some of which give magical aid (helpers). When he arrives at the nadir of the mythological round, he undergoes a supreme ordeal and gains his reward. The triumph may be represented as the hero's sexual union with the goddess-mother of the world (sacred marriage), his recognition by the father-creator (father atonement), his own divinization (apotheosis), or, again—if the powers have remained unfriendly to him—his theft of the boon he came to gain (bride-theft, fire-theft); intrinsically it is an expansion of consciousness and therewith of being (an illumination, transfiguration, freedom). The final work is that of the return. If the powers have blessed the hero, he now sets forth under protection (emissary); if not, he flees and is pursued (transformation flight, obstacle flight). At the return threshold the transcendental powers must remain behind; the hero re-emerges from the kingdom of dread (return, resurrection). The boon that he brings restores the world (elixir)" (Joseph Campbell, *HWTF*, pp. 245-46).

of the mentally disturbed or in the literary creations of contemporary writers. For, if both the universal myth and the personal dream present analogous situations and are symbolic in the same way of the dynamics of the psyche, in the dream and the work of art *the archetypal forms are reshaped and transformed* according to the peculiar problems or obsessions of the dreamer or artist, while in myth the problems and solutions offered are equally valid for all men. The variations each author proposes when he omits or embroiders around the basic design are highly indicative, then, of the configuration of his own psyche.

Schema III covers the different stages of the hero's adventures, whether "positive" or "negative." While the "positive" quest presents the adventures of the mythological hero *par excellence* (that is, the "elect" youth, beloved of the gods, whose character has been embellished with all the virtues: courage, truthfulness, and chastity among the most important), there is also a "negative" quest, which presents the adventures of a hero whose character is tainted by several flaws, especially a defective spiritual "vision" or an excessive pride. This hero, then, must experience a far more terrible chain of adventures meant to "purify" his character before he can attain to the ultimate revelation. Yet, he might rebel against divine order and undertake the "infernal" way which leads to the destruction or dissolution of the self, rather than to harmony. There are many examples to illustrate the "negative" way; one is the popular—and probably apocryphal—episode of Heraclitus' immersion in dung—mentioned in the climax to Part I of *Rayuela*—as a prerequisite to the final illumination. Similarly, Lucius Apuleius' *The Golden Ass* relates the successive degrading episodes the hero must undergo before attaining a glimpse of Queen Isis, who returns him to his human shape and thus allows his "return" to the world of men. The Romantics, and particularly the Symbolists, dealt with the concept of the "negative" quest more than any of their predecessors; their works developed the concept of a ritual that violated the traditional aims of the rites of initiation by aiming at a detachment of the hero *from* society, rather than his integration within it. The Symbolists were acquainted with esoteric doctrines and made ample use of occult symbolism; but one of their main models was Poe, the Poe of *Pym* and the tales of the sea. Both Rimbaud's "Le Bateau ivre" and Baudelaire's "Le Voyage" elaborate upon Poe's pattern of a journey through mystic horror, vertigo, and wonder through which the soul is prepared to encounter a final illumination. But—and this is again an important characteristic of the "negative" initiation—the "negative" journey rarely ends, in Poe's sea stories, with the third stage, or the hero's "return" (only in "A Descent Into the Maelström" is such a return achieved). Its final aim seems to be the destruction of the self at the moment of revelation and the total annihilation of the personality in the attempt to merge into total unity. This characteristic is best exemplified in *Pym*. By the time the Baron de Huysmans wrote his decadent masterpiece, *A rebours*, the sacred or spiritual aim of the quest had lost much of its importance; in his novel, the initiation into a world of degradation and darkness simply becomes a means to chase away boredom by recurring to more and more daring transgressions; the symbolic Grail is no longer sought and has become, in fact, forgotten or irrelevant. The quest becomes merely a quest for the excitement or horror of the *adventure*, with no end in mind.

Turning now to a consideration of the mythic structures observable in Poe's *Narrative of Arthur Gordon Pym* and Cortázar's *Rayuela*, I shall attempt to show the extent to which these novels depart from the basic initiatic pattern, and I will venture an interpretation of what these deviations imply. Moreover, I hope to show the extent to which Poe's concept of the "negative" quest influenced Cortázar's own.

In the "negative" quest pattern, exemplified by Poe's *Narrative of Arthur Gordon Pym*, the hero does not undertake the quest through a decision of his own, but is almost "pushed into it." Pym starts out his adventure as a boyish prank; he gets drunk and, in this state of total abdication of the will, drifts out to sea. Here, he experiences the whole depth of horror inspired by the stormy sea at night and by the shipwreck. Unable to achieve a return counting on his own resources, he must be "rescued." Poe does not present the spiritual symbolism of Pym's adventures in a haphazard fashion; he meticulously constructs a network of allusions that evince his control of the total symbolic scheme at work through a constant reinforcement of ideas presented from the beginning.

Pym's first voyage—the "call" to the quest—is undertaken when Augustus and Pym succumb to a sudden, magnetic attraction for the sea after listening to stories of sea adventures. Augustus becomes strangely transformed and swears with a "terrible oath," longing for the "glorious breezes from the southwest." Later, Pym himself is "possessed," springs from his bed "in a kind of ecstasy," and thinks "this mad idea one of the most delightful and most reasonable things in the world." As they sail, he becomes frightened when gazing upon Augustus' transfixed face under the light of the moon and asks him to turn back:

> . . . it was nearly a minute before he made answer, or took any notice of my suggestion. "By and by," said he at length—"time enough—home by and by." I had expected such a reply, but there was something in the tone of these words which filled me with an indescribable feeling of dread. (*Pym*, p. 15)

His dread is metaphysical; it responds to what Pym senses *beyond* the voyage, rather than to the perils of the voyage itself at this point. As soon as Pym decides to undertake the quest ("I recommended myself to God and made up my mind to bear whatever might happen with all the fortitude in my power. Hardly had I come to this resolution, when . . . ," *Pym*, p. 7), he undergoes the first initiatic death and resurrection as the *Ariel* is run over by a larger ship, and the sailors in it rescue him and Augustus. Poe, once more, stresses the miraculous character of his hero's rescue, attributing it to good fortune or to what "the wise and pious . . . [call] the special interference of Providence" (*Pym*, p. 19). In this first voyage—the voyage of the *Ariel*, which, with her owner Augustus, appears as the supernatural helper—Pym undergoes the first initiation or ordeal: the experience of extreme horror.[2] In the first initiation, the hero must be pushed to extremes; Pym, who longed for apocalyptic visions, has his fill ("It is hardly possible to conceive the extremity of my terror," *Pym*, p. 16). In the beginning of Chapter 2, Pym confirms his commitment to the quest; nothing can interest him but the memories of his adventures at sea, and he longs *precisely* for more dreadful, horrible adventures:

> My visions were of shipwreck and famine; of death or captivity among barbarian hordes; of a lifetime dragged out in sorrow and tears, upon some gray and desolate rock, in an ocean unapproachable and unknown. . . . I regarded them only as prophetic glimpses of a destiny which I felt myself in a measure bound to fulfill. (*Pym*, pp. 22-23)

The second initiatory ordeal demands that the hero, having experienced himself to the fullest, go beyond himself in a move of solidarity towards another or towards a group. Poe is very meticulous in his account of this second ordeal. The dates are faithfully recorded. The departure of the ship belonging to Augustus' father where both youths plan to stow away had been set for June 15. Pym enters the hold where he is to hide (the initiatic cave) on June 17; but the ship does not actually depart until three or four days later, that is, on *June 20 or 21*. The date is, indeed, of crucial importance; it marks the summer solstice and is very close to the Eve of Saint John—June 24—both traditionally associated with magic, rites of fertility, and the temporary return of the dead. Most importantly, this is the date when the sun enters the sign of Cancer; Orphic teaching sees Cancer as "the threshold through which the soul enters upon its incarnation."[3] It is traditionally a date chosen for initiation rites. Cancer, moreover, is governed by the Moon "in the performance of its symbolic role as mediator between the formal and the informal worlds."[4] Likewise, the sign of Cancer is associated with sacrificial deaths; in *The Golden Bough*, we are told that the priest-king was slain every twelve years, as Jupiter entered Cancer. Pym's confinement and experiences of hunger, thirst, and terror correspond to the primitive's initiatory ordeals, meant to bring about the "death" of the outgrown personality and the "birth" of the new one.

The name of the second ship is also symbolic; it is named *Grampus*; that is, it contains an allusion to the Wise Old Man whom the hero meets as "helper" along the quest. If the hero is sympathetic towards the "helper," he will partake of the Old Man's wisdom. If not, he will experience the Old Man's revenge. Pym passes the test of "solidarity" when he intervenes in the struggle between the mutineers and Augustus' party by disguising himself as the swollen corpse of a poisoned mate. Now he meets the hybrid Dirk Peters, who will soon take the place of Augustus as Pym's double and helper. With Peters' company, Pym undergoes the "trials" characteristic of the second stage of the quest, which ends when both are rescued by the *Jane Guy*.

The third stage—the meeting with the goddess as prerequisite to the "return" —begins when the captain suddenly announces his decision to change course and descend to Antarctica. Up to this point, the narrative had displayed a rather conventional style; now, we are confronted by a highly elaborate symbolic scheme, consisting primarily of a play with symbols of "light" and "darkness" and the utilization of geographical personifications to suggest the all-embracing presence of the Magna Mater. The third stage of the quest tests the hero's ability to distinguish between illusion and reality and demands that he "lift the veils" from the goddess's face and be able to gaze into the truth that hides behind it; this means he must be able to withstand the revelation of the mystery and accept truth without being destroyed by it. Only then can the hero return to the world and heal his fellow men with the "elixir" or wisdom he has gained.

Pym descends to a labyrinthine cavern with mysterious hieroglyphs engraved on its walls; in this cavern (symbolic in itself of the chthonic Earth Mother who, as Goddess of Death and Mistress of the Dead, presided over the rituals of initiation and death that took place in similar caverns), he meets the shrouded White Figure. Pym's journey ends here, as the hero sails past the "veil" of the cataract towards the blinding light emanating from the figure:

March 22. The darkness had materially increased, relieved only by the glare of the water thrown back from the white curtain before us. Many gigantic and palidly white birds flew continuously now *from behind the veil*, and their scream was the eternal *Tekeli-li!* as they retreated from our vision. . . . And now we rushed *into the embraces of the cataract*, where a chasm *threw itself open to receive us*. But there arose in our pathway a shrouded human figure, very far larger in its proportions than any dweller among men. And the hue of the skin of the figure was of the perfect whiteness of the snow. . . . (*Pym*, p. 185; my italics)

The date, March 22, marks the rites of spring, the mysteries of the Great Mother, the goddess Anna Perenna. The chasm is personified to suggest the body of a goddess; the cataract appears as the veil that hides her. If we refer once more to Schema II, we find, under the category "death mysteries," the recurring fantasies and visions appearing in the unconscious of a person possessed by the archetype of the Terrible Mother. The ending of *Pym* suggests the archetypal mysteries of death associated with this figure. *Pym*, as we saw, had exerted a significant influence over the conception of Cortázar's earliest novels; the motif of the rites of death, the descent to the nether world, and the meeting with the Goddess of Death and Mistress of the Dead became internalized thereafter, reappearing at the climax of *Rayuela*.

Oliveira, like the hero of the "negative" quest, rejects the tradition and refuses to accept the roads for fulfillment it offers. He sees his attitude as a result of "haberse negado desde temprano a las mentiras colectivas o a la soledad rencorosa del que se pone a estudiar los isótopos radioactivos o la presidencia de Bartolomé Mitre" (*R*, p. 31). Only the desire to reject society and the whole social and intellectual tradition of the Occident is clear in his mind; he does not know, however, what he has to find. In a later chapter, he defines his "method" when he tells Gregorovius: "Hay que dar vueltas alrededor como un perro buscándose la cola. . . . No renuncio a nada, simplemente hago todo lo que puedo para que las cosas me renuncien a mí" (*R*, p. 216). His method, then, is essentially passive. The archetypal hero actively undertakes a number of adventures and battles strewn in his path by various adverse spirits; the antihero, likewise, undertakes a journey into a realm of darkness and horror. Oliveira, however, simply lets things happen, refusing to take any definite stand in any of the situations where he finds himself. The author, however, expects an active role from his readers. Cortázar—through his persona Morelli in the third part of the novel—gives the reader a theory that accounts for both his character's attitude and his own attitude as a writer. He states that his novel is deliberately ambiguous for, rather than presenting the reader with a definite emotion or theory, he gives him "como una fachada, con puertas y ventanas detrás de las cuales se está operando el misterio que el lector cómplice deberá buscar (de ahí la complicidad) y quizá no encontrará (de ahí el copadecimiento). Lo que el autor de esa novela haya logrado para sí mismo se repetirá (agigantándose, quizá, y eso sería maravilloso) en el lector cómplice" (*R*, p. 454). The "lector macho," then, must search for those answers that the hero—and the author—have declined to pursue and present. If we combine Morelli-Cortázar's statement with Horacio's, we have a definition that somewhat resembles that of the antiquest: it is a passive quest where the hero rejects the traditional "way"; it is an unconventional presentation on the part of the author, who offers no definite answers. Yet, the author expects an active role from the reader, who is supposed to find a "clue" or "key" in the novel's very formlessness, which supposedly conceals some kind of "hidden order."

It has been rightly observed that most of Cortázar's critics have approached *Rayuela* by the same routes the author prepared for them in his declarations about the novel and in the Morelli chapters.[5] In them, Cortázar observes that the inconclusiveness of the novel is deliberate, as are its ambiguities and contradictions. And yet, must we blindly accept an author's judgement of his work and overlook the deeper implications of the contradictions in it simply because the author says that he was presenting them according to a preconceived plan? I agree with Jaime Concha when he observes that the ambiguities in *Rayuela* really respond to a basic indecision in the project itself and to the feeble ground upon which Cortázar's novelistic architecture has been erected.[6] The explanations thus far accepted by the majority of his critics, I would add, must be carefully dealt with and not valued for more than what they appear to be when juxtaposed to the achievements of the novel itself: *a posteriori* argumentations. I believe the development of the novel is hindered by the author's refusal to confront the archetypal symbolism in la Maga and fathom its implications.

La Maga, as we saw in the preceding chapter, acts as "anima" or supernatural helper throughout the first eight chapters of *Rayuela*. By living in complete opposition to the cultural canon, she illustrates the way *à rebours* that Horacio can only approximate conceptually. Their meetings—like those events that determine the stages of Pym's quest—are ruled by a strangely meaningful series of chances and moments of inspiration. Similarly, their contacts throughout the first eight chapters could best be described as "ecstatic." Oliveira, however, does not undergo an experience comparable to Pym's extremity of horror. His encounters with la Maga are really disencounters; he avoids love by standing one step away from his actions ("hacíamos el amor con un virtuosismo desapegado y crítico," *R*, p. 24) and by labeling his feelings "mere desire" in order to resist giving in to them and to retain his detached position ("Puesto que no la amaba, puesto que el deseo cesaría [porque no la amaba, y el deseo cesaría], evitar como la peste toda sacralización de los juegos," *R*, p. 44). Finally, he protects himself by denying la Maga's very presence, thus turning the act of love into a grotesque parody ("La Maga no sabía que mis besos eran como ojos que empezaban a abrirse más allá de ella, y que yo andaba como salido, volcado en otra figura del mundo, piloto vertiginoso en una proa negra que cortaba el agua del tiempo y la negaba," *R*, p. 27). The last metaphor is of crucial importance; it suggests that Oliveira rejects la Maga for the sake of that other quest, where he acts as "a vertiginous pilot on the black prow of a ship which divides the waters of time, denying them." The mentions of vertigo (whirlpool, maelstrom), a black ship ("MS. Found in a Bottle," "A Descent into the Maelström"), and the refusal of time (the philosophical dialogues, *Eureka*) remind us of Poe; most likely, Oliveira/Cortázar sees that "other" quest as Poe's, Baudelaire's, and Rimbaud's: as a rejection of the accepted collective canon and as a head-long plunge into a realm of darkness, hoping for a discovery of "le nouveau" and for the purification of the soul.

However, if Oliveira sees la Maga as an obstacle in his spiritual journey, why does the author describe her, in fact, as the synthesis of everything Oliveira seeks? Why is the initial chapter (73), which alludes to a metaphysical quest, relegated to the "disposable" section, while the novel itself begins with the question "¿Encontraría a la Maga?" Why does the quest of the "kibbutz of desire"—the symbolic concretion of Oliveira's metaphysical longing, his "Cave of Quietude"—disappear altogether in the second part of the novel, while the two climactic chapters (41 and 52) deal with Oliveira's attempts to recover la Maga, and his last thoughts, while he balances himself on the windowsill, about to jump, center again on la Maga? Why is the first part of *Rayuela* so strikingly similar to André Breton's *Nadja*,[7] a novel dealing with the poet's search for a woman in whom he sees the concretion of his search for the absolute? Few critics have asked themselves these questions; most have accepted the explanations provided by the narrator, that is, that Oliveira abandons la Maga because he must continue his "quest," and he feels that la Maga will hold him back (*R*, p. 339). One wonders how the sheepish, inarticulate, and overly complying Maga could hold the hero back even from a walk in the rain, let alone from a spiritual quest—unless the braces are to be found in the hero himself. In *Rayuela*, Cortázar communicates to his hero Oliveira his own constellation of the Feminine, that is, the threatening *image of woman as Parsifal's mother*, who attempts to prevent her son from leaving her side and setting out on the quest. Here, we find the first and basic indecision in the conception of the novel: the author presents la Maga in the first chapters of the novel as "anima," or as the inspiring and guiding figure who entices the hero to adventure and discovery, and whose secrets he is to decipher, comprehend, and absorb. Yet, there is an unconscious resistance on the part of the author regarding his character. That feeling prevents him, apparently, from carrying out his original project. Instead, he aims at the presentation of the scene where Oliveira is to desert la Maga. Let us examine how the author's duality toward his character is manifested in the novel.

We have seen that in the first stage of the quest, the hero must undergo an experience of extreme intensity in whatever realm or area of experience he has chosen. Thus, Pym undergoes an extreme experience of terror; Endymion, one of passion. These experiences are meant to let the hero "know himself" by experiencing his own nature to the fullest. There is no comparable experience regarding Oliveira and la Maga; the scenes previously quoted betray the radical *distance* the hero keeps between himself and the experience his body—detached from his self—carries out with la Maga. There is one unusually intense scene in Chapter 5 ("una larga noche de la que luego hablaron poco," *R*, p. 44). But, rather than acting as a turning point and as a step leading to a different stage in their relationship (as Lycius' cruelty towards Lamia, for instance, had brought about), this experience changes nothing; Oliveira, in fact, fears the altering of their relationship. The same static quality defines his intellectual functions; Oliveira possesses "una conciencia más atenta a no dejarse engañar que a aprehender la verdad" (*R*, p. 32). Thus, neither in the sensuous nor in the intellectual plane does he undergo the extremes of "intensity." He rejects la Maga and proceeds, then, to the second stage of the quest: the test of "solidarity" or "compassion," where the hero must forget himself facing his fellow humans' griefs.

As he decides to leave la Maga behind in order to pursue his quest, Oliveira encounters two possibilities of showing "solidarity." The first is the Morelli incident: Oliveira witnesses the accident where an old man is run over by a car. Later he hears that the man who suffered the accident is a writer and that he is alone. He feels inclined to pay the man a visit, but postpones the project. He makes the visit only after Rocamadour's death and then, as Morelli offers the key to his apartment (and to his manuscripts), Oliveira declines the responsibility, letting Etienne take "esa llave a la alegría, un paso a algo que admiraba y necesitaba, una llave que abría la puerta de Morelli, del mundo de Morelli" (R, p. 628). Morelli plays the symbolic role of the Wise Old Man who gives the hero the "key" or potion or magic word that will facilitate his victorious outcome in the "tests." But if Morelli truly possesses "the key" to the world that corresponds to Oliveira's authentic longings, why does the latter postpone the visit until after Rocamadour's death? Oliveira finally asks Etienne to accompany him on his visit to Morelli, and in that same conversation, he tells Etienne about his recent nightmare. In the nightmare, a piece of bread cries when he cuts it; this is, evidently, a dramatization of his guilt regarding the baby's death. Since the whole episode occurs in the "disposable" section and Oliveira ends by surrendering the key to Etienne, the Morelli episode appears as a *compensation*, on Oliveira's part, for his failure to manifest his feelings for the baby and la Maga. Immediately following this episode (and intimately related to it, regarding the nature of the "test" they represent), comes the Berthe Trépat episode.[8]

Horacio had used the expression "to rain" in order to symbolize his desire for an overflow of emotion that would make him "tener lástima de algo" (R, p. 117), thus allowing him to escape from the emotional desert where his soul has wandered. Now he walks in the rain, looking for an "inner rain" as well. Then he enters the confined, stifling, cavelike theater where Berthe Trépat's concert takes place. The hero's spiritual malaise, the role of chance in his choice of the theater, and the initiatic quality of the dark, stifling theater stress the suggestion of a "passage" in this episode. Berthe Trépat appears, then, as the "helper" under the guise of Wise Old Woman, or as the mystagogue of the second stage. There is a curious parallel between Pym's meeting of the hybrid Peters aboard the *Grampus* in the second stage of his quest and Oliveira's meeting of Berthe Trépat at this point. Both are particularly deformed, grotesque figures. The hybrid Peters is described as:

one of the most ferocious-looking men I ever beheld. He was short in stature, not more than four feet eight inches high, but his limbs were of Herculean mould. His hands, especially, were so enormously thick and broad as hardly to retain a human shape. His arms, as well as legs, were *bowed* in the most singular manner. His head was equally deformed, being of immense size, with an indentation on the crown . . . and entirely bald. . . . The mouth extended nearly from ear to ear; the lips were thin, and seemed, like some other portions of his frame, to be devoid of natural pliancy, so that the ruling expression never varied under the influence of any emotion whatever. (*Pym*, p. 48)

Berthe Trépat's description shows a significant similarity with that of Dirk Peters; she is likened to a "marionette," an "automaton," a "clown" (*R*, pp. 126-27). All her movements are sudden, geometrical, mechanical. There are touches in her description that remind us of Jarry ("tenía un aire entre guerrero y Ubu Roi," *R*, p. 134). Like Jarry in *Le surmâle*, Hoffmann in "Automata" and "The Sandman," and Poe in "Maelzel's Chess Player," Cortázar here displays an almost morbid fascination with masks and automatons. Berthe Trépat represents the grotesqueness man is capable of reaching when he has lost contact with the natural processes of life and has severed communications with the rest of men. Everything contributes to create an impression of "falseness" in Berthe Trépat's description: the automaton movements, the masculine shoes not concealed by the feminine skirt or the ribbons, the masklike face. There is no humanity left in this marionette who has lost all contact with mankind through her own obstinacy. Like Peters, she is deformed and "hybrid"; her music, the "sincretismo fatídico," is a reflection of herself, a fateful syncretism of dead attitudes and ideas, temporarily animated and on the verge of dissolution. There is, however, an essential difference between Berthe Trépat and Dirk Peters: the latter's *strength*. When Pym helps Peters overcome the mutineers—in spite of the initial fear and repulsion he had felt for the man—he passes the second test and is rewarded with the help of his companion. An alliance seems to be, then, established: Pym acquires Peters' strength, while Peters partakes of Pym's "humanity." Pym/Peters become, together, a complete entity, able to undertake the third and final stage of the quest. Together, like Don Quixote and Sancho Panza, they form a body/mind organism of two mutually dependent sides.

This is not the case with Oliveira/Berthe. Oliveira fails to rescue Berthe Trépat from her puppetlike condition because he does not really sympathize with her or grieve for her. Pym overcomes his initial repulsion for Peters and wins his help. Oliveira, on the contrary, feels such a repugnance for Berthe Trépat that he almost abandons her during their walk in the rain ("Es repugnante, habría que tirarla contra un escalón y meterle el pie en la cara, aplastarla como a una vichuca, reventarla como un piano que se cae del décimo piso. . . . Le tengo asco, yo me rajo en la esquina que viene, total, ni se va a dar cuenta," *R*, p. 136). If he later stays with her, it is only because he derives an unexplainable joy mixed with hope from the idea of accompanying the pianist to her apartment and meeting her husband, Valentin. The episode of Berthe Trépat, particularly Oliveira's strange excitement—a mixture of joy and hope—in the midst of it, poses one of the greatest problems of interpretation in the whole novel and has long puzzled Cortázar's critics. I believe there is a significant connection between this episode and those that immediately precede and follow it.

Oliveira has announced his intention to leave la Maga and her sick child, even though he still seems to love her. He finds an opportunity to gain "entrance" to Morelli's world, but foregoes it. Then he meets Berthe Trépat, toward whom he attempts to show the "solidarity" he had failed to express toward la Maga and her child. Yet, it is not Berthe Trépat herself he sees; as they walk in the rain, it soon becomes evident that la Trépat is so wrapped up in her own world that she is hardly aware of Oliveira's presence. Meanwhile, he begins, as well, to elaborate his own fantasies. It is very significant that in these fantasies, Oliveira associates Valentin with Rocamadour. As Berthe Trépat mentions one of Valentin's tantrums, he thinks: ". . . trataba de imaginarse a Valentin llorando boca abajo en la cama, pero lo único que conseguía era ver a un Valentin pequeñito y rojo como un cangrejo, en realidad veía a Rocamadour llorando boca abajo en la cama y a la Maga tratando de ponerle un supositorio y Rocamadour resistiéndose y arqueándose, hurtando el culito a las manos torpes de la Maga" (*R*, p. 138). The identification between Valentin/Rocamadour immediately suggests a subtler, more terrifying association for Oliveira: that between la Maga and Berthe Trépat. Berthe Trépat now displays her overbearing, "castrating" side; she seems to bear the blame for Valentin's homosexuality. La Maga, envisioned in the act of applying a suppository to Rocamadour, is given a parallel role. Her action suggests sodomization; she appears to be blamed for Rocamadour's "sodomization," as Berthe Trépat seems to be for Valentin's. The joy and hope Horacio feels when he visualizes the scene at the pianist's house arise from his association of both situations; it is as though he were given the chance to "rescue" Valentin/Rocamadour and, by extension, magically suppress the threat that hangs over himself through the presence of la Maga:

> la alegría había sido tan nueva, tan otra cosa, y *ese momento en que a la mención de Valentin* metido en la bañera y untado de caca de gato había respondido *una sensación como de poder dar un paso adelante, un paso de verdad,* algo sin pies y sin piernas, *un paso en mitad de una pared de piedra*, y poder meterse ahí y avanzar *y salvarse de lo otro,* de la lluvia en la cara y el agua en los zapatos. (*R*, p. 144; my italics)

"Lo otro," evidently, is not only the rain on his face and the water in his shoes; it is also Valentin's condition, homosexuality, by which he feels threatened in every castrating figure of Woman, perceived basically as an avatar of Parsifal's mother. The identification between Berthe Trépat and la Maga becomes explicit at the end of the episode; Berthe Trépat is no longer a ridiculous puppet, but becomes transformed into a towering, despotic, and indeed "terrible mother" figure who slaps, insults, and ridicules Oliveira in front of her neighbors. At this very moment, he thinks:

> Miraba el corredor a oscuras, revolviendo los ojos, la boca violentamente pintada removiéndose como algo independiente, dotado de vida propia, *y en su desconcierto Oliveira creyó ver de nuevo las manos de la Maga tratando de ponerle el supositorio a Rocamadour*, y Rocamadour que se retorcía y apretaba las nalgas entre berridos horribles. . . . (*R*, p. 148; my italics)

I believe that the tremendous relevance of this episode in deciding the course of Oliveira's later behavior can be traced to the hero's subtle, unconscious identification between himself/Rocamadour/Valentin and la Maga / Berthe Trépat / the Terrible Mother under the guise of Parsifal's mother. When Berthe Trépat denies him access to her apartment (and with it, the opportunity of "rescuing" Valentin), she crushes with one blow all his hopes for redemption and liberation from the castrating image of Woman he carries inside himself and projects on the women that approach him. Later, as he walks in the rain, he thinks:

> Es demasiado idiota, pero hubiera sido tan bueno subir a beber una copa con ella y con Valentin, sacarse los zapatos al lado del fuego. . . . Te falló, pibe, qué le vas a hacer. Dejemos las cosas así, hay que irse a dormir. No había ninguna otra razón, no podía haber otra razón. Si me dejo llevar soy capaz de volverme a la pieza y pasarme la noche haciendo de enfermero del chico. (*R*, p. 150)

His desire, at that instant, to go and care for the child is still related to his former desire to "rescue himself" during the Berthe Trépat episode. Later, when he finally returns to la Maga's room, that redeeming feeling will no longer be there. Then he acts as though he knew that all his efforts to save the child had been useless, for the lot had been drawn long ago. Only his hidden hatred and resentment against la Maga remain. The only way to "save" the child is, then, to let him die.

If the separation from a mother figure—such as the one Oliveira seems to project on la Maga, for she is the provider of his spiritual nourishment, and he "starves" when she leaves—is involuntary and not the result of the hero's decision, it is no separation at all; only the presence goes, but the essence remains and becomes even more overpowering than before. Pym had undertaken the quest through an *active* decision, of his own will. But Oliveira acts, throughout the novel, *by default*. After la Maga leaves, Oliveira literally falls apart, dissolves his former ties, abandons his projects, succumbs to nightmares and depressions: "Allí donde esté tiene el pelo ardiendo como una torre y me quema desde lejos, me hace pedazos nada más que con su ausencia . . ." (*R*, p. 225).

However, since Oliveira's need of la Maga is still inhibited by his dread of her "terrible" aspect, he fails to look for her when Wong gives him the address where she can be found. Once more, the author recurs to cynicism to explain his hero's refusal to look for la Maga, whose presence he so anxiously desired. Oliveira says: "yo en realidad tendría que ir. Una cierta obligación estética, completar la figura. El tres, la Cifra. Pero no hay que olvidarse de Orfeo . . ." (*R*, p. 238). Indeed, we must not forget Orpheus, who descended to Hades in pursuit of his lost Eurydice and *was killed and dismembered by the maenads* upon his return. Thus, the apparently cynical statement gives us, as if through a slip of the mind, the deeper reason behind Horacio's refusal to look for la Maga.

Once the preliminary tests are past, Pym undertakes, with Peters' company, the descent to the cave of the White Figure; his action marks the final stage in his quest (since Poe omits the stage of Father-atonement and the apotheosis and return). Oliveira prepares himself, next, for the following stage in the quest, through which he apparently compensates for his refusal to undertake the *other* descent to which la Maga had challenged him.

For Oliveira—as for Pym—the last stage is seen as a descent into a realm of darkness and horror; he undertakes this part of his journey at midnight, in the midst of a "noche de empusas, lamias, mala sombra" (*R*, p. 238). He goes through all the ritualistic motions: he crosses a bridge (symbolic of "passage") and descends to the "Lethe," the banks of the Seine. His peculiar "Hades" is the world of the *clochards*, whose lives illustrate, as well, a "negative" quest. In the figure of the *clocharde*, we find an explicit connection with Berthe Trépat: physically, she possesses, as well, an "Ubu Roi" air about her which is both ridiculous and threatening. Like Berthe Trépat, she responds to Oliveira's friendly advances by practically "glueing" herself to him. Like the pianist, she is a cumulus of madness, inhumanity, and degradation. The understated connection between Berthe Trépat and la Maga is made explicit in the case of the *clocharde*: she hints at a somewhat equivocal relationship between herself and la Maga, which seems to make them, in Oliveira's eyes, "two of a kind" (the motif of the old witch and the young sorceress who are one and the same is a common one in mythology and will reappear in *62*, in the parallel between Frau Martha and Hélène). But the *clocharde* is much more: it is she who appears as a Magna Mater *travesti*. She becomes Oliveira's mystagogue in the Hades of the *clochards* and, later, "initiates" him through a rather peculiar form of *hieros gamos*:

Oliveira veía las placas de mugre en la frente, los gruesos labios manchados de vino, *la vincha triunfal de diosa siria* pisoteada por algún ejército enemigo, una cabeza criselefantina revolcada en el polvo, con placas de sangre y mugre *pero conservando la diadema eterna a franjas rojas y verdes. La Gran Madre tirada en el polvo y*

pisoteada por soldados borrachos que se divertían en mear contra los senos muti-
lados, hasta que el más payaso se arrodillaba entre las aclamaciones de los otros, el
falo erecto *sobre la diosa caída*.... (*R*, p. 246; my italics)

But as in the episode of Berthe Trépat, the "initiation" ends in punishment
and deprivation as the police interrupt the "ritual" taking place between
Oliveira and the *clocharde* and hurl both of them into a paddy wagon.
Still, Oliveira achieves a kind of "return" after this episode, for he is deported
back to Buenos Aires.

Poe's novel had deviated from the archetypal structure of the quest by
omitting the third stage, the return, and ending the novel at the very moment
when the hero confronted the Magna Mater in the cave of Tsalal. Cortázar's
previous novels, similarly, had ended with Andrés Fava's confrontation with
Death (*El examen*) and Medrano's death in the labyrinth (the Medrano episode
at the end of *Los premios*). Now, for the first time in Cortázar's novels, the
hero achieves a return. But this is no return at all, since, like Horacio's separation from la Maga, it is not *voluntary*. In reality—as the narrator himself
declares (*R*, pp. 268-69)—Horacio *is returned*. And so it happens that instead
of the further rituals by which the hero is to readapt himself to the world he
returns to, Oliveira continues his former quest—the search for la Maga (*R*,
pp. 336-39)—having forsaken his former metaphysical speculations and literary
ambitions. He now parodies the rites of social integration: he starts living
with Gekrepten (marriage), he takes a job (assumption of a role in adult
society), and so on. Yet, since he has not achieved an *authentic* return, the
quest continues in a more tortuous manner, now in a subliminal level. Tension
between the two levels at which Horacio then functions builds up until it is
resolved in the parallel episodes that bring Part II of the novel to a climax:
Chapters 41 and 52.

In both, Talita—Traveler's wife—plays a central role. Now she has become
la Maga's double and, as such, the Magna Mater who must "initiate" Oliveira.
Both chapters are the exact opposite of one another in a symbolic sense. In the
first, which suggests the "diurnal" world, the one to which Horacio has supposedly returned, Talita rejects Horacio, choosing her husband, Traveler, as the
two men stand on opposite sides of an improvised bridge, awaiting her choice.
Yet, Oliveira feels that "la negativa a pleno sol podía quizá ser otra cosa a
plena noche" (*R*, p. 320). And indeed it is. The rejection in "life" or "day"
turns into acceptance in the midst of darkness, in the kingdom of the dead.
The "third initiation" is repeated, but no longer parodied, in Chapter 52, as
Horacio descends to the morgue of the insane asylum and kisses la Maga, who
has returned through Talita, showing pity for Horacio and sadly smiling to him
as if accepting his suffering.

The polarities of these two episodes are synthesized in the juxtaposition of
a number of elements in them.[9] These polarities are presented in Schema IV.

Chapter 41	*Chapter 52*
CIRCUS–controlled games	ASYLUM–games no longer controlled
TENT–opening pointing upwards, outside	LIFT–opening pointing downwards, inside
BROAD DAYLIGHT–consciousness	MIDNIGHT–mystery, the unconscious
HEAT–action, life	COLD–death
BRIDGE–a passage	MORGUE–surrender, defeat, death
HEIGHT–consciousness	BASEMENT–the unconscious

SCHEMA IV–Polarities in Chapters 41 and 52 of *Rayuela*.

The chapter of the morgue is a symbolic descent to the underworld, a visit to the unconscious. It reproduces the crucial scenes in *El examen* and *Los premios* previously analyzed. The overwhelming appeal of Death, not expressed openly after *El examen*, reappears now at the climax of *Rayuela*. Oliveira longs to fall, to be absorbed by la Maga, who, as Death, returns through Talita. As in *Pym*, this is the ultimate revelation: afterwards, Horacio prepares a symbolic "defense" in his room and loses his mind, or leaps from the window.

Another diagram can synthesize the basic parallels I have discussed up to this point regarding *Pym* and *Rayuela*. These parallels are presented in Schema V.

In spite of their similarities, then, the two novels are essentially dissimilar, since Cortázar's hero lacks the *commitment* to the quest which is present in Poe's. Oliveira's quest, in fact, represents an entirely modern phenomenon: the counter-initiation. René Guénon describes the counter-initiation as a more or less deliberate enterprise in which a counter-hero defends those modern ideas that represent only the negative antitradition and presents them as an apparently coherent system and a preparatory stage for the coming of a more "positive" existence.[10] The representatives of the antitradition (the "negative" quest) had presented isolated phenomena or merely marginal movements which

	PYM	*RAYUELA*
1ST INITIATION (intensity)	extreme terror	emotion withheld
SUPERNATURAL HELPER	*Ariel*—Augustus	la Maga
2ND INITIATION (solidarity)	Pym helps Peters' party	Oliveira rejects involvement
WISE OLD MAN / WOMAN	*Grampus*; Peters as mystagogue	Morelli, Berthe Trépat; *clocharde* as pseudo-mystagogue
3RD INITIATION (acceptance of reality)	Pym descends to the South Pole	Oliveira descends to Buenos Aires
MEETING WITH THE TERRIBLE MOTHER; LIFTING OF THE VEILS .	white animals with red fangs and claws; "Tekeli-li," "Anamoo-moo"; White Figure, cave—DEATH	"el perro"; ghost of la Maga; morgue—DEATH, MADNESS
ENDING	novel unfinished	novel inconclusive

SCHEMA V—Parallels between *Pym* and *Rayuela*.

never transcended the boundaries of the intellectual milieu; the hero of the counter-tradition concentrates and exteriorizes all the satanic influences of the past and is characterized by an irresistible, charismatic attraction. He embodies the promise of a "spiritual restoration" and the reintroduction of qualitative differences in a world suffering from an excess of materialism and homogeneity; but his will be "une hiérarchie inversée, c'est-à-dire proprement une 'contre-hiérarchie,' dont le sommet sera occupé par l'être qui en réalité touchera de plus près que tout autre au fond même des 'abîmes infernaux.' "[11] This hero, even when he appears under the guise of a particular character, is less of an individual than a symbol: "il n'aura dans ce rôle ni prédécesseur ni successeur; pour exprimer ainsi le faux à son plus extrême degré, il devra, pourrait-on dire, être entièrement 'faussé' à tous les points de vue, et être comme une incarnation de la fausseté même."[12] The hero of the counter-initiation proposes a greater order, but all he actually presents to allude to that order is a synthesis of dead, faded attitudes. He is made up of animated remnants of various ideologies or attitudes towards life which lack a central, authentic center. And, as Guénon observes, "cet amas de 'résidus' galvanisé, si l'on peut dire, par une volonté 'infernale,' est bien, assurément, ce qui donne l'idée la plus nette de quelque chose qui est arrivé aux confins mêmes de la dissolution."[13] Guénon observes that the hero of the counter-initiation will not have any predecessor or successor. However, Nikolai Stavrogin from Dostoievsky's *The Possessed* seems to have antedated Oliveira in this role and fits perfectly into Guénon's description of the counter-hero. Philip Rahv observes that, in creating Stavrogin, Dostoievsky reached "the last frontier of modern imagination, and it is perhaps for this reason, since life did not yet contain him, that he could not make him 'true to life,' but was forced to rely almost entirely on his mastery of the devices of melodrama and mystification."[14] Cortázar does make Oliveira "true to life," for the counter-hero is no longer unknown to our time but is, on the contrary, its product. But perhaps Cortázar was also thinking of Stavrogin when he created Oliveira, for he admitted—during our first interview—that he had reread *The Possessed* in the early sixties.

The similarity between Oliveira and Stavrogin is very meaningful indeed: Stavrogin is the first representative in literature of the archetype of the Antichrist. The word for the Antichrist (Mesîkh) is a deformation of the name for the Messiah (Mesîha).[15] Moreover, "mesîkh" means "deformed," a word that gives us the essence of what the archetype represents. Oliveira's actions in the second part of *Rayuela* appear, in fact, as a deformation of Traveler's, whose first name is, significantly, Manuel. The counter-initiation, being a deformation of everything the initiation is supposed to accomplish, leads to the disintegration of the personality, rather than to its harmony. The Antichrist must be as near as possible to this state of "disintegration"; his individuality—developed in a "monstrous" or "deformed" manner—is also on the verge of annihilation or dissolution by means of suicide or madness, "réalisant ainsi l'inverse de l'effacement du 'moi' devant le 'Soi,' ou, en d'autres termes, la confusion dans le 'chaos' au lieu de la fusion dans l'Unité principielle."[16]

We have seen that the fixation and predominance of the Terrible Mother archetype throughout Cortázar's early writings reaches its climax in *Rayuela*, a novel whose structure is built around successive encounters with different manifestations of this archetype. *Rayuela* ends after a climactic descent to a "cave of the dead" and a numinous encounter with a Magna Mater figure. The hero of the novel, on the other hand, has a highly numinous character in himself, since he seems to represent the archetype of the Antichrist. Erich Neumann observes that "behind the archetype of Satan and the blackness surrounding him, at whose impact the crumbling world of the old cultural canon has collapsed, rises the devouring Terrible Great Mother, tearing and rending and bringing madness. And everywhere in modern art we see this dissolution in the breakdown and decay of form."[17] The predominance of the Terrible Mother archetype is an expression of the total disintegration of the old cultural canons in our society; the appearance of Satanic heroes and Terrible Mother figures in the literary works of the past century and a half responds to the annihilation of all that was formerly held to be good and true and to the destruction of what was held to be "real." The contemporary artists, no longer trusting appearance and the rational processes of causal association, adopted the methods of free association directed by unconscious process; by these means, they abandoned the disintegrated former "reality" and plunged into the collective unconscious in search of new forms, new truths with which to order the external chaos. Distortion, crookedness, and grotesque horror form an archetypal aspect of the demonic; thus, if our times are ruled and determined by the Terrible Mother archetype of the collective unconscious, the symbolism arising from the depths of the author's psyche is bound to reflect this state of chaos by presenting her. Hence, as Neumann observes, we misunderstand the art of our time if we regard its relation to chaos as purely negative; a conscious renunciation of form does not arise from incompetence or from inability to give form, but from the artists' belief that, by leaving the directive process of creation to chance, they might discover a greater truth arising from the depths of the collective unconscious, for "it is precisely in chaos, in hell, that the New makes its appearance. Did not Kwanyin descend into hell rather than spend her time with the serene music makers in heaven?"[18]

Cortázar's novel cannot justly be said to constitute a plunge into the New, into the abysmal depths of the collective unconscious; publishing his novel in 1963, the author had already faced a "tradition" of demonic literature from which he drew a number of models: Stavrogin can be discerned behind Oliveira; Nadja behind la Maga; Jarry's characters behind Berthe Trépat and the *clocharde*; the Surrealists, the Symbolists, and Poe behind the concepts of the negative quest and the creative process ruled by chance. The author's acquaintance with the very Jungian concepts discussed above inhibits a purely "unconscious" plunge into the world of the archetypes. The peculiar manner in which he fashioned and weaved these various influences into the symbolic scheme in *Rayuela* is, still, his own. The character of la Maga, in particular, which has exerted such a magnetic fascination on the novel's critics, is Cortázar's own product, in spite of its similarities with Nadja or Aurélia or its kinship with the Jungian concept of the "anima." In her, the author seems to have conceived, however falteringly, a "new" archetype, a synthesis—in the character's "primitive" mentality and sensitivity—of the mind/body dualities at the heart of his previous creations and, indeed, of our century's art. La Maga becomes the center of the novel and the object of Oliveira's quest from the first scene ("¿Encontraría a la Maga?" *R*, p. 15) to the last ("lo único que él podía hacer era mover un poco la mano derecha en un saludo tímido y quedarse mirando a la Maga, a Manú, diciéndose que al fin y al cabo algún encuentro había . . . ," *R*, p. 404), and she recurs in a muted manner in subsequent works (Feuille Morte in *62*, Lina in "Lugar llamado Kindberg"). But here is where we find the root of the feeling of stagnation and futility in Cortázar's later works:[19] once the author plunges into the world of the collective unconscious and becomes subject to the numinous currents arising from the archetypes that become constellated in his own unconscious, he must confront the message and the meaning embodied in these archetypes. Cortázar enters a dead-end road through his refusal to confront the meaning embodied in the archetype in *Rayuela* and in subsequent novels. If André Breton failed to decipher the message embodied in *Nadja*, he returned to the confrontation of the symbolism of the Feminine in *L'amour fou* and, finally, in *Arcane 17*. But Cortázar externalizes his resistance to the archetype by presenting, in *62*, a gagged Feuille Morte and a monstrous Hélène *whom the hero refuses to see* ("Preferí no saber, aunque hubiera podido," *62*, p. 262) and by avoiding the archetypal Feminine altogether in his latest novel, *Libro de Manuel*.

Once an author chooses to be guided by the forces of the unconscious, he cannot avoid, without facing dire consequences, the confrontation with the symbolic figures that are born through him. This is, indeed, one of the basic principles of depth psychology.[20] If the symbol is not confronted, it causes a dissociation of the psyche which is manifested, among other ways, in a feeling of futility and falseness; in Neumann's words: "We must face our own problems and our own imperfections; and at the same time we must integrate a superabundant outward and inward world that is shaped by no canon. This is the conflict that torments modern man, the modern era, and modern art."[21] Cortázar's refusal to elucidate the meaning behind the symbolic figures in *Rayuela* must be pointed out, I believe, as a major cause for the feeling of futility (at times veiled with missionary zeal) in his later works, in spite of his conscious attempts at change and renovation.

4

The Collective Quest

In *Rayuela*, Cortázar developed the theme of the personal or individual quest further than ever before in his writings. However, the inability to proceed after the moment when his hero faced a confrontation with the symbolic figure of the Magna Mater apparently induced him to decline the discussion of individual destinies in subsequent works. In *62*, he explored the problem of "figures" or collective destinies; in *La vuelta al día en ochenta mundos* and *Ultimo round*, he began to display an interest in the collective concerns of mankind which was destined to attain larger proportions in his later works. In a letter to the Cuban writer Roberto Fernández Retamar, later published in *Ultimo round* (*UR*, lower level, pp. 199-210), Cortázar stated that his awareness of the achievements of the Cuban Revolution and of the political awakening in Latin America had coincided with the turning point in his development as a writer; Cuba's plight, he claims, made him realize the relevance of Latin America's political problems to the individual destinies of every Latin American.

The question of Cortázar's political involvement has been extensively dealt with by various critics.[1] I do not intend to add further arguments to those discussions, since they are not relevant, in any case, to the issue I am dealing with at present. Cortázar's comments about Keats's relationship to politics, however, suddenly become very pertinent indeed. In his book on Keats, Cortázar had implied that Keats's concern with developing a "staid Philosophy" with which to confront the problems of mankind had stemmed from a desire to buttress himself against the impending threat of annihilation or dissolution of the self he had felt in the character of his passion for Fanny Brawne. According to Cortázar's interpretation, *Hyperion* hides, under the overt theme which evinces Keats's concern for mankind's destiny, an undercurrent of meaning revealing Keats's own personal problem. It is curious to notice that after the completion of his book on Keats, Cortázar does not refer to the English poet again until 1967, precisely at the time when he begins to demonstrate his own concern with collective issues. The political allusions in *La vuelta al día* might seem superficial and even frivolous to many; yet in the article that closes the book and seems to define his position, the author anticipates the criticism his new attitude might provoke. This article is called "Casilla del camaleón," and it reproduces, with no significant alterations, a fragment from Chapter 10 of *Imagen de John Keats*, written fifteen years earlier.

In "Casilla del camaleón" Cortázar affirms that only the mediocre or unimaginative succeed in eliminating contradictions from their political outlooks and in taking firm stands regarding the concrete issues at stake; but the "chameleon poet" reserves to himself the right to exist in the midst of "mysteries, uncertainties, doubts." Cortázar discusses Keats's "chameleon letter"—to Woodhouse, 27 October 1818—and concludes:

> Llegado el caso—no hay más que leer su correspondencia—Keats era tan capaz como cualquier otro de tomar partido . . . ; pero ese sentimiento de esponja, *esa insistencia en señalar una falta de identidad* . . . apuntan a ese camaleonismo que nunca podrían entender los coleópteros quitinosos. (*VDOM*, p. 211; my italics)

The selectiveness of Cortázar's memory becomes very revealing; in limiting his discussion of Keats's attitude to the "chameleon letter" of 1818, he overlooks the whole process of Keats's development which culminated in the views that shaped *The Fall of Hyperion: A Dream* and are dramatically expressed in several sections from his letters, such as the following one, a letter to George and Georgiana Keats (21 April 1819), where he exclaims:

> There may be intelligence or sparks of the divinity in millions—*but they are not Souls [the] till they acquire identities*, till each one is personally itself. I[n]telligences are atoms of perceptions—they know and they see and they are pure—in short they are God—*how then are Souls to be made? How then are these sparks which are God to have identity given to them*—so as ever to possess a bliss peculiar to each one's individual existence? *How, but by the medium of a world like this?* [My italics][2]

We have now come full circle back to that moment in his book on Keats when, after a discussion of *Hyperion*, Cortázar had concluded that Keats's nature rejected the theory of "knowledge" that his reason dictated but that his senses were opposed to. After this discussion Cortázar seems to have "blocked" the ideology of the mature Keats, discussing his poetics—in Chapter 10 of *IJK*—merely on the basis of "chameleonism" and "negative capability." Now, in "Casilla del camaleón," he concludes that "la íntima seguridad que tiene Keats de su plenitud interior, la confianza en su intrínseca humanidad espiritual . . . lo liberan tanto del narcisismo confesional a lo Musset como de la oda al libertador o al tirano" (*VDOM*, p. 213). And yet Keats, while avoiding easy praises of the then "fashionable" political stands—as Cortázar states—*did* embrace political commitments in his lifetime, even in the early days of his career, when he supported the liberals who gathered around the figure of Leigh Hunt and thus provoked the anger of the conservative-controled *Blackwood Magazine* and *Edinburgh Review*. But most importantly, Keats insisted on a relentless lucidity upon confronting the real world with all its sufferings, pettiness, and contradictions; he would be destroyed in the attempt to "die into life" rather than maintain an attitude that he believed false. Keats had always expressed sympathy for the views that presented the progress of mankind as a collective movement that involved every member of the society, and thus the views expressed in *Hyperion* are not essentially foreign to his internal ideological development. This attitude becomes especially prominent after the walking tour to Scotland and is expressed in several of the letters written at this time.[3]

In spite of the oversimplification with which Cortázar had dismissed Keats's political attitude in "Casilla del camaleón," the true nature of Keats's position seems to have haunted him; the ghost of *Hyperion* and *The Fall*—the very works that had so shaken Cortázar at the time when he wrote *IJK*—reappear, twenty years later, at the background of two climactic scenes in Cortázar's "political" novel, *Libro de Manuel*. At this moment, Cortázar faced a number of issues analogous to those Keats had confronted when embarking on the first and second versions of *Hyperion*; perhaps unconsciously, he seems to have revived his earlier identification with Keats.

It has been observed that *Hyperion* was written during a critical period in Keats's life when the poet felt he was "dying" to a former existence and "being reborn" to a new personality.[4] The illness and death of Keats's younger brother Tom represented, in a way, a threat to that younger, more naive poetic self which had delighted in the pure and uncommitted enjoyment of the pleasure "bowers." *Hyperion* is organized around the concept of the defeat of the older, chthonic gods and the rise of Apollo, god of light and reason, who must be "initiated" to godhead. *Hyperion* has two main levels of meaning: firstly, it represents a personal initiation in which the Keats who believed in "negative capability" and delighted in a self-centered enjoyment of life's pleasures is to die and be reborn as the mature Keats who has attained "knowledge enormous." Secondly, it presents a more general discussion of every poet's responsibility regarding the whole of mankind as a race. At this time, Keats was under the influence of the ideas expressed by Wordsworth in *The Excursion* about the growth of the poet's mind and his need to abandon the stage of egotistical concerns and attain awareness and "knowledge" of the problems that affect the whole race.

After a vague and at times hesitant and even forced beginning, Keats presents, in Book III of *Hyperion*, the scene where Apollo, who has contemplated the grief of the downstricken, vanquished race of Titans, must be *initiated* to godhead by undergoing a confrontation with Mnemosyne, the goddess of memory. In this section of his poem, Keats alludes to one of the most ancient rituals of the pre-Olympic Greek mythology that centered on the images of *female* deities; in presenting such an unconventional mythological allusion, Keats seems to have been responding to a deeper impulse that somehow associated with the archetypal initiation into the concerns of a community, with a more personal problem, that of his relationship to women. The theme of the confrontation with the figure of a Wise Woman, moreover, constitutes, in terms of depth psychology, an indication of the onset of a period of profound transformations of the personality; since the woman is not presented as a "terrible" or devouring figure at first, it can be said that this is regarded as a "positive" transformation. The aim of the primitive rites of initiation to the goddess Mnemosyne was that of strengthening the bonds between the individual and the tribe's past, for as Jane Harrison observes in her discussion of the rites to the goddess of memory, "all consciousness is memory . . . all consciousness is in anticipation of the future . . . consciousness is above all a hyphen, a tie between the past and the future."[5] In her function of providing a link between the past and the future, the goddess Mnemosyne possesses a symbolic value analogous to that of the Divine Child, and she announces what Jung calls the process of *integration* of the personality. The initiation rite Apollo must face, accordingly, corresponds to the third stage of the quest where the hero must accept "reality" before achieving his "return" to mankind, according to the classification earlier introduced. If the first stage tests the hero's capacity for intensity of feeling and the second, his capacity to feel solidarity for the rest of men, the third initiation tests the hero's ability to distinguish between appearance and reality, and his capacity to accept reality. Apollo must now face the supreme test: confronting the goddess Mnemosyne and explaining to her the *meaning* of the actions he has witnessed.[6] The goddess says:

> Tell me, youth,
> What sorrow thou canst feel; for I am sad
> When thou dost shed a tear: explain thy griefs
> To one who in this lovely isle hath been
> The watcher of thy sleep and hours of life
>
> . . . .
> Show thy heart's secret to an ancient Power
> Who hath forsaken old and sacred thrones
> For prophecies of thee, and for the sake
> Of loveliness new born.
>
> (III, ll. 68-72; 76-79)

Apollo asks, in his turn, " 'Why should I tell thee what thou so well seest / Why should I strive to show what from thy lips / Would come no mystery' " (III, ll. 84-86). According to the previous discussion about the symbolic value of the different stages of the quest, what the third initiation tests is precisely the ability to attain to "consciousness" or "knowledge" by explaining what was previously seen or felt. Keats, however, cannot proceed after this point in his poem; the third book breaks off at the moment in which Apollo gazes into Mnemosyne's face after she symbolically "lifts the veils" that had covered it. Still, this symbolic third stage of the initiation became the central theme of Keats's last two longer poems: inability to distinguish between illusion and reality becomes the tragic flaw that occasions Lycius' ruin; the ability to distinguish between the poet and the dreamer and the acceptance of the former's destiny becomes a precondition, in *The Fall of Hyperion: A Dream*, for the Poet's accession to the shrine of Moneta/Mnemosyne.

In *The Fall of Hyperion: A Dream*, Keats attempts to accomplish the symbolic third stage of the quest once more; now, he has abandoned the distance and grandeur of the earlier, Miltonic version and adopts a more direct approach by presenting himself as the Poet—rather than presenting the god Apollo, as in the earlier version—who is to die to a previous selfish and unknowing self and be reborn through his capacity to feel and understand the sufferings of mankind. Dorothy van Ghent relates the rituals enacted in these two poems to the Orphic ritual where the initiate had to sink "beneath the bosom of Despoina" in order to be reborn; she observes that Keats seems to be deliberately archeological in the presentation of this event in *The Fall*.[7] In the latter version we do find, indeed, a profusion of symbols that were absent from the earlier presentation of the initiation. If in the previous version Keats had merely spoken about the goddess's robes and veils, he now presents the Poet drinking a sacred beverage made with honey (I, ll. 42-46; the bee was the Orphic symbol of wisdom). He then enters a vast sanctuary with a high, domed ceiling, shrouded in perennial darkness (an initiatic cave, I, ll. 81-86). Next, he ascends the steps of the shrine (a "mystic ladder" symbolizing the different stages in the purification of the soul) and advances toward the veiled figure (I, ll. 131-38) who addresses him thus:

> None can usurp this height . . .
> But those to whom the miseries of the world
> Are misery, and will not let them rest.
> All else who find a haven in the world,
> Where they may thoughtless sleep away their days,
> If by chance into this fane they come,
> Rot on the pavement where thou rotted'st half.—
>
> (I, ll. 147-53)

If the image of Apollo's deification through "knowledge enormous" had come to Keats as in a dream or a vision, the process of the Poet's deification is more humanlike; unlike Apollo, whose brain was flooded with knowledge without any effort on his part, the Poet must attain to knowledge through successive degrees or stages of understanding, as the goddess Moneta explains to him the meaning of the ritual. After the Poet ascends the steps, overcoming the numbness of his limbs and a nightmarelike terror, he asks the goddess why he among men has been granted entrance into her shrine. The goddess then introduces a first classification of men, dividing them in two groups: those who sympathize with the world's sufferings and those who spend their lives in an animallike contentment (I, ll. 147-53). The ones who "feel" are, in their turn, divided into those who are nonvisionaries ("They seek no wonder but the human face; . . . They come not here, they have no thought to come . . . ," I, ll. 163-65) and the dreamers. The goddess expresses her contempt, then, for the dreamers; she compares the Poet with the nonvisionary "men of feeling," telling him "thou art less then they":

> What benefit canst thou do, or all thy tribe,
> To the great world? Thou art a dreaming thing;
> A fever of thyself—think of the Earth;
> What bliss even in hope is there for thee?
> What haven? every creature hath his home;
> Every sole man hath days of joy and pain,
> Whether his labours be sublime or low—
> The pain alone; the joy alone; distinct;
> Only the dreamer venoms all his days,
> Bearing more woe than all his sins deserve.
>
> (I, ll. 167-76)

Since the poet is divorced from the rest of men and even from nature, from the Earth, he cannot find happiness but in a realm that, in a way, answers the longing of his dreams. Yet, he has been admitted into this realm *because* of the agony he has felt for the sufferings of mankind. Then we are introduced to a third distinction: the visionaries form two groups, the mere dreamers and the true poets:

> The poet and the dreamer are distinct,
> Diverse, sheer opposite, antipodes.
> The one pours out a balm upon the world,
> The other vexes it.—
>
> (I, ll. 199-202)

With this distinction, Moneta's speech ends; now the Poet's transformation is to take place. I shall not engage in a discussion of the canceled fragment and its bearing on the meaning of the poem.[8] I believe that with or without the canceled fragment, Keats identifies the Poet's previous condition as that of a "dreamer" who "venomed all his days" without heeding humanity. Through Moneta's revelation, the Poet dies to his former self and emerges as a true poet, attempting henceforth to achieve the task entrusted to him in the ritual, which is the ordeal by which he transcends mental darkness and attains consciousness. The Poet's death and rebirth takes place as the ritual reaches

its climax with the "parting of the veils" from Moneta's face. The goddess
appears to possess the complexity of the maternal archetype to which Keats
seems to have been so sensitive. But rather than stressing any of her particular
aspects, Keats presents her in her awesome multiplicity: as the Good Mother
("As near as an immortal's sphered words / Could to a mother's soften, were
these last," I, ll. 249-50) and as the mysterious, almost inhuman Terrible
Mother who transfixes and paralyzes:

> Then saw I a wan face,
> Not pin'd by human sorrows, but bright blanch'd
> By an immortal sickness which kills not;
> It works a constant change, which happy death
> Can put no end to; deathwards progressing
> To no death was that visage; it had pass'd
> The lily and the snow; and beyond these
> I must not think now, though I saw that face—
> But for her eyes I should have fled away,
> They held me back, with a benignant light,
> Soft-mitigated by divinest lids
> Half-closed, and visionless entire they seem'd
> Of all external things—they saw me not,
> But in blank splendor beam'd like the mild moon,
> Who comforts those she sees not, who knows not
> What eyes are upward cast.
>
> (I, ll. 256-71)

Moneta synthesizes and transcends opposites in her multiplicity. She is both
loving and indifferent, and is likened to the moon because of her remoteness
and mystery, as well as her all-embracing and yet detached character. The
Poet feels urged to penetrate the mysteries of Moneta's brow; significantly,
the images used to manifest the Poet's urge to know are aggressive and violent:

> As I had found
> A grain of gold upon a mountain's side,
> And twing'd with avarice strain'd out of my eyes
> To search its sullen entrails rich with ore,
> So at the view of sad Moneta's brow,
> I ached to see what things the hollow brain
> Behind enwombed: what high tragedy
> In the dark secret Chambers of her skull
> Was acting. . . .
>
> (I, ll. 271-77)

The Poet's apparent longing to penetrate the archetypal Mother's entrails
and appropriate her secret wisdom with "avarice" presents a situation analogous to the archetypal episode of "being swallowed by the monster" or by
the Earth Mother that typifies a number of primitive rites of passage;[9] in such

episodes, the hero must kill the monster in order to break free. As Morris Dickstein rightly observes, the relationship with the goddess figure in *The Fall* implies "no regression, as happens frequently in *Endymion*, to the infantile position at the breast, as a refuge from consciousness. On the contrary, this is an independence and selfhood, achieved through destructive appropriation."[10] The Poet finally achieves a transformation when he is inspired by the desire "To see as a God sees, and take the depth / Of things as nimbly as the outward eye / Can size and shape pervade . . ." (I, ll. 303-06). He discovers his true mission as one who will indeed reject illusions for the sake of reality, though not "reality" as understood by the other categories of men Moneta enumerated, but rather *the whole depth of reality* that has not yet been explored by man: "the poet, he realizes, is a humanist not by abjuring consciousness but by exploring new forms of consciousness."[11] Knowledge, for him, seems to be finally defined as a combination of rationalistic discipline and the instinctual powers of man which, combined, will maintain a necessary bond with the Earth. Contrary to Cortázar's belief that Keats had abandoned both versions of *Hyperion* because his inner nature rejected the path that his reason dictated, I believe that here Keats attained— for once, if only briefly—an equilibrium between the affective and the ratiocinative, the conflict of which had formerly caused his inner division. The poems break off, I believe, because his consciousness was "flooded" by the irruption of ideas or "visions" that overwhelmed him, being too numerous for him to integrate in such a brief period of time. But his repeated returns to the same themes and situations show his willingness to decipher the "messages" that had come to him in the form of visions and point, in *The Fall*, to an acceptance and a harmonious integration of *knowledge* into his view of poetry. By choosing the Keats of chameleonism and "negative capability," the Cortázar of *La vuelta al día* and before gives us an indication of his own views regarding the poet's position facing the world. Yet, for the Cortázar of a few years later—the one who faced, in *Libro de Manuel*, a number of issues analogous to those that Keats had tried to confront in *Hyperion* and *The Fall*—the dream of the Poet in *The Fall* and the complexity of the attitudes symbolized in it seem to have held a special fascination.

In the prologue to *Libro de Manuel*, Cortázar declares that this book presents a synthesis of his experiences regarding the political problems of Latin America and the culmination, at the same time, of his personal quest for meaning and for the integration of his personality (*LM*, p. 7). This work, then, holds a similar place in Cortázar's development as the two *Hyperion*s had regarding Keats. Keats had instinctively conceived of a ritualistic central scene in order to convey the whole depth of meaning in the transformation he experienced; Cortázar, likewise, presents the vision of his hero's transformation by means of *a ritualistic dream* in which the hero is symbolically prompted to accept "reality" and adopt a clear position regarding the rest of the world, both in the personal and the social levels: ". . . el sueño de Fritz Lang de alguna manera incomprensible era al mismo tiempo una forma diferente y oscura de ese callejón sin salida pero con el doble nombre de Ludmilla y Francine . . ." (*LM*, p. 166). Cortázar's novel, however, does not present the totality of the experience that is to be confronted in the complexity of the figure of the dream; in his dream, the figure is an unidentified man simply referred to as "the Cuban," with what appears to be a conscious political intent on the part of the author. Yet the dream is meant to carry a deeper meaning than a mere allusion to the central character's need to define his political stance. The author employs a second symbol that represents, like Keats's Moneta/ Mnemosyne, the conjunction of opposites the ritual is meant to achieve; this is the symbol of the child Manuel, who corresponds to the Jungian archetype of the Divine Child and announces the onset of a period of positive transformation culminating in the conjunction of opposites. M. Esther Harding observes that the child symbolically born of the initiation "is the symbol of the new individuality, which is brought to birth through inner experiences."[12] Cirlot sees the child as the symbol of the future, while the Old Man was the symbol of the past: "the child is of the soul—the product of the *coniunctio* between the unconscious and consciousness: one dreams of a child when some great spiritual change is about to take place under favorable circumstances."[13] The Divine Child, then, has a symbolic value analogous to that of Moneta, which, according to the Jungian view, represents "the true Self with which Keats can at last integrate his ego, or more limited selfhood."[14]

Andrés Fava—the main character in *Libro de Manuel*—undergoes a symbolic initiation rite in what he later calls "the Fritz Lang dream." This initiatic sequence holds a great number of similarities with, but also significant differences from, the ritualistic dream in *The Fall*. In "the Fritz Lang dream," Andrés finds himself in the darkness of a movie theater (an initiatic cave acting as a modern and desacralized shrine), is led away from the picture of a screaming woman on. the screen, traverses a number of dark, labyrinthine corridors, and ascends the steps that lead to an encounter with "the Cuban." Outwardly, the two dreams present a number of similar settings and actions. Yet, the heroes respond in a rather dissimilar way. The Poet in *The Fall* had actively pursued an encounter with the veiled figure; Andrés Fava *is led* to the Cuban almost by accident. Moneta/Mnemosyne inspires a very complex reaction in the Poet; he dreads her revelation, yet feels comforted by her motherly voice, and while appalled in the face of her supernatural stature, decides to penetrate her mysteries and longs to attain the wisdom she possesses. Andrés Fava's reaction in the dream only denotes sheer terror and rejection. He does not overcome, like the Poet, the numbness of his limbs in a heroic gesture of acceptance, but defends himself by forgetting the words uttered by the Cuban in the dream. Thus, if in Keats's poem the Poet had prepared himself for the revelation by the anguish of the journey and the revelations in

Moneta's speech, in Cortázar's novel Andrés Fava confronts the figure of the Cuban with no previous preparation and avoids facing the meaning of the words that would enable him to accept a confrontation with his deeper self. He succumbs to a feeling of horror and for some time blocks the words in the dream. He does not remember the Cuban's words ("Wake up") until after he has performed a second ritual (the rape of Francine) and questioned another masucline Mnemosyne (Lonstein).

The sequence of the rape of Francine (mistress #2) takes place after Ludmilla (mistress #1) abandons Andrés Fava. Ludmilla, disenchanted with Andrés' infidelities and his inability or reluctance to develop a less selfish relationship (their alliance is described as a pact between two "allied narcissists"), falls in love with Marcos, a member of the clandestine organization "la Joda" (the Screw Job) and the prototype of the uncomplicated, devoted political activist the author places in juxtaposition to Andrés, as if approving and repeating Moneta's indictment of the Poet: "thou art less than they." Ludmilla leaves Andrés in order to join the Screw Job and her new lover. Andrés is deeply distressed at the news of Ludmilla's decision and immediately looks for Francine to cry on her shoulder over the loss of Ludmilla. Together, they visit the prostitution district of Paris, the most sordid strip-tease joints, and various other territories with varying degrees of bleakness. Suddenly, Andrés falls into a trancelike state similar to that experienced by Andrés Fava in *El Examen* after the death of the nameless youth or by Medrano near the end of *Los premios* when encountering Bettina's "ghost" or by Oliveira in the chapter of the morgue in *Rayuela*, where he is visited by the "ghost" of la Maga. Andrés now seems to look upon Francine as the gate through which he can attain the revelation he has so far failed to achieve, and as the means to regain, somehow, the lost Ludmilla. Andrés seems to punish Francine for what Ludmilla has done to him and intends—like the hero in "Ligeia"—to recover Ludmilla by means of his torture and degradation of Francine.

There seems to be a contradiction here between the author's expressed intention and his actual accomplishment. The rape is presented as an attempt on Andrés' part to "erotically liberate" Francine—who, meanwhile, does everything within her power to resist the "liberation." Andrés later claims that Francine was, indeed, a willing accomplice and that she longed to be treated exactly thus. Yet, Francine announced her decision to trade Andrés—liberation included—for a ski week-end in the Alps (*LM*, p. 288). Still, we might accept the rape *per angostam viam* and even the preceding events as incidents to be classified under the rubric of "erotic liberation." But the scene where Andrés forces Francine to look at the tombs in the Montmartre cemetery as they copulate would appear a bit irregular even to the most liberally minded. It is important to define the character of this action, for it is *precisely by means of it* that Andrés attains the revelation which had formerly escaped him:

". . . algo en mí había visto del otro lado, había como una cifra final del inventario, un balance acabado, sin palabras ni conductas que seguir: un brusco cumplirse, un quebrarse de ramas" (*LM*, p. 293). What has Andrés Fava understood through his ritual of sadism and necrophilia? Why can he remember the words of the Cuban *only* after this episode?

There is a very meaningful connection between Andrés' sadistic attack on Francine, his encounter with Lonstein, and "the Fritz Lang dream": all three have a "dark" aspect in them and imply a rejection of Woman and the glorification of a masculine figure. Lonstein is openly linked with the spirit of Poe; there are playful allusions to the rue Morgue, Fortunato and Montresor (the protagonists in Poe's "The Cask of Amontillado"), and other sinister situations during the evening in which Lonstein—in the midst of an uncommonly necrophiliac spree—gives a detailed account of his duties and obligations at the morgue. And Marcos describes his tirade as "tu Edgar Poe al alcance del pueblo" (*LM*, p. 36). Cortázar, who never wholly broke away from his youthful fascination with Poe, yet feared the implications of such an identification, makes Andrés Fava confront his own sadistic "other self" through the rape of Francine and through the encounter with the necrophiliac Lonstein before he can remember the dream and complete the "initiation."

Cortázar's previous novels—from *El examen* to *62*—had presented climactic scenes closely related to those in "Ligeia" and *Pym*, as we have seen; the hero, undertaking a symbolic "descent" to the nether world, encountered Woman as the representative of Death and was torn apart by the confrontation. *Libro de Manuel* is the first novel by Cortázar where woman does not play such an awful, overpowering role. In fact, the women in this novel appear as the most schematically drawn feminine characters in Cortázar's novels, while the "supernatural" aura is projected on a masculine figure, the Cuban in the dream. For the first time, the male hero is able to overcome Woman as Death in the episode of Francine's rape while facing the Montmartre cemetery. The rape of Francine is preceded by a psychological "descent" (the visit to the prostitution district), the crossing of a bridge (symbolic of passage), and the entrance into the kingdom of the dead (the hotel facing the Montmartre cemetery). By raping Francine, Andrés Fava liberates himself from the overpowering threat of death which had crushed his namesake in *El examen* and his literary relatives in the other novels by Cortázar.[15] Having defeated woman, Andrés Fava proceeds to the next stage in the quest: the atonement with the Father.

Significantly, the symbolic role of Father is given, in this novel, to a *Poesque* figure: Lonstein. In her study *The Parental Image: Its Injury and Reconstruction*, Dr. Esther Harding observes that when a child is in any way forsaken by a parent (whether abandoned, allowed to go hungry or ill, or otherwise neglected), as Cortázar had been, he tends to regard that parent as a "wicked" figure; yet, he is compelled, at the same time, to imitate the "mythicized" figure of that parent. When this kind of situation is produced, the individual remains inwardly bound to the parent, in a negative sense; but nonetheless bound to that "wicked" parent, for hate binds as much as love—and sometimes more. He then develops an unconscious, mythicized image of that parent in its most ideal form, unchecked by the limitations that would arise from a confrontation with a real situation, while directing his aggressiveness against the actual parents and/or *all they represent.* In Dr. Harding's words:

> . . . he longs for parental love and clings to an image of an "ideal" parent that no real human being could possibly fulfill. But outwardly he fights the real parents and the parental image whenever he finds it, projected possibly to a human being, or perhaps to an institution. He becomes one of the group that Neumann has characterized as the "strugglers"—people who are ever in rebellion, but who never achieve a definite victory, either over the parents or over their own childishness.[16]

The only way to heal this trauma is to dissolve the negative image by projecting the positive parental image on a human being who will be able to tie, again, the bonds of trust and faith that had been severed.[17] As Jung observes, "What has been spoiled by the father can only be made good by a father. . . ."[18] An ordinary man might project the Good Father image on the analyst; but the creative writer, whose work becomes, indeed, the very agent of his process of transformation, projects this image on a character with whom his literary persona must come to terms. In Cortázar's *Libro de Manuel*, this role is performed by Lonstein.

Cortázar adorns Lonstein with Poesque characteristics; Poe had been, we might recall, the figure with which the child Cortázar identified in his earliest literary attempts, and Poe had remained Cortázar's most important master in the early years of his career, teaching him his first "lessons" in literary theory and practice. The love-dread attitude towards the "Poe-shadow" had already appeared in "El otro cielo"; but *Libro de Manuel* achieves a resolution of the previously accumulated tension in a moment of encounter and recognition.

As Andrés and Lonstein meet, a series of ritualistic actions are again performed: Andrés ascends the steps of the apartment where he meets Lonstein, and both proceed to clean the body of Manuel (the Divine Child; the soul); they drink together, and as they return to the living room, Lonstein proceeds to question Andrés as to the reasons behind his quest for Ludmilla and the Screw Job:

> . . . al final los tres volvieron al salón con un gran sentimiento de confraternidad y buena conciencia. El que te dije anotaría más tarde que ese intervalo un tanto coprológico y urinario había tenido su importancia porque Lonstein le dio un vaso de grapa a Andrés y seriamente, casi solemnemente, le preguntó qué carajo pretendía con eso de los datos sobre Verrières. . . . (*LM*, p. 341)

Andrés' actions mirror those in the dream and seem to "actualize" the message in it. In the dream, Andrés abandons the theater where a woman screamed on film; now, he leaves the "screaming" Francine behind. In the dream, he wanders amid narrow corridors and reaches the precinct where the Cuban waits. Now, after he has wandered around the streets of Paris and reached Lonstein's apartment, he is told, as in the dream, to "wake up" and realize that "las mujeres también tenían su triangulito que decir" (LM, p. 344). We are now ready to speculate upon why the author named this dream "the Fritz Lang dream."

The very mention of Fritz Lang—most famous for his cinematic portraits of arch-criminals, such as Dr. Mabuse, M, and Dillinger—already suggests the atmosphere of darkness, murder, horror, evil forces, and obsessive wanderings through dark, labyrinthine streets associated with the settings of "El otro cielo," the episode preceding Francine's rape, and, indeed, Poe's murder stories. However, after a careful consideration, I have concluded that the film alluded to in this particular context is neither M nor any of the Dr. Mabuse series, but rather Metropolis.[19] Indeed, in this film we find a synthesis of both the overt themes of Keats's The Fall and Cortázar's Libro de Manuel and an underlying level of psychological allusion to the dread of the Feminine and the theme of atonement with the Father; it combines, then, personal and transpersonal factors.

The basic relationship between the film and the initiatic dream in The Fall—reflected in Andrés Fava's dream—is to be found in the theme of the poet who is born to an awareness of mankind's sufferings and performs the role of mediator between mankind and the powers above. At the beginning of the film, Freder Fredersen—the protagonist—is seen in a typical idyllic "bower," the "Eternal Garden," where he sports in the company of aristocratic friends among fountains and peacocks; suddenly, he is visited by Maria, one of the workers' daughters, who appears surrounded by children and whose name already suggests the inspiring role of the "anima." She entices him to descend to the bowels of the earth, to the Workers' City, telling him, as she points to the children: "These—these are your brothers." Freder is smitten by Maria's words and seems to wake up from a long dream; he descends to the Workers' City, and there, as he helps a worker who has fainted from exhaustion by taking his place at the machine, he undergoes the test of "solidarity." He has earned the right to descend further into the catacombs, where "She" speaks, and a fellow worker invites him to follow him. As she leads the workers in prayer and they fall on their knees, Maria exhorts: "Between the brain that plans and the hands that build, there must be a mediator. It is the heart that must bring about an understanding between them." Freder—like the Poet in Keats's poem—feels that this role is destined for him.

Here we have, then, the basic similarities that Cortázar apparently sensed in Keats's and Lang's "dreams" as he combined elements from both to create his own initiatic dream. There is, however, another and more important element in the movie: the nightmare Freder suffers after he is deceived by the robot built to resemble Maria. Rotwang, the evil inventor at the service of Jon Fredersen, Freder's father and Master of Metropolis, makes a robot in the image of Maria, but embodying the opposite qualities of those she possesses: the false Maria is sensuous, deceitful, violent. As he irrupts into his father's quarters, Freder beholds a sensuous, bewitching Maria enticing his father. The sequence that follows is, I believe, the particular scene Cortázar refers to when he mentions "the Fritz Lang dream." In it, Freder, overcome by the emotions of the scene he has witnessed, faints and sinks into a delirious state, represented by a series of visual effects: a blinding light advances towards Freder, a whirl-pool effect "swallows" him, Freder "falls" into the darkness and envisions the image of Death swinging a scythe and advancing towards him. . . . In his delirium, Freder sees a sensuous, almost obscene Maria attired in veils and a half-crescent headdress, as an evil goddess enthroned on top of snakes and wild animals, driving men to frenzy and madness. If the first "dream" in the film had illus-trated the overt, transpersonal intention in Cortázar's novel (i.e., the regenera-tion of mankind), this dream sequence synthesizes the basic personal fears manifested in the climactic scenes in his previous novels by presenting the "terrible" side of the Feminine in the form of the evil goddess of death and madness. Moreover, the dream suggests the Oedipal situation of rivalry with the Father over Woman and the anxiety resulting from a fear of punishment. Later, as the robot is destroyed, the archetypal stage of atonement with the father takes place in the film. The workers, at the instigation of the false Maria, have destroyed the machines of Metropolis; as a result of this acton, the whole city is flooded ("flooding," we have seen, symbolizes the irruption of unconscious forces). Later, the workers find out it was Jon Fredersen's son who saved their children from drowning, and a confrontation takes place. The master of the ruined Metropolis and the bearded foreman who leads the workers reach out, but hesitate and fail to clasp hands. Maria then pleads: "There can be no understanding between the hand and the brain unless the heart acts as media-tor." Freder then clasps his father's and the foreman's hands in each of his hands, and all three become reconciled: hand, heart, and brain will rebuild Metropolis.

It is evident that the symbolic scheme of *Metropolis*—integrating, as it does, a number of Cortázar's central concerns—played an important role in the over-all symbolism of *Libro de Manuel*. While the film reflects the basic transper-sonal meaning of Keats's *The Fall*, it also introduces an important figure absent from Keats's poem: that of the Father. After meeting Lonstein (atonement with the Father), Andrés plays a similar role as "mediator" between the attitude of the revolutionaries and that of—Lonstein? The latter seems to perform, indeed, the role of the "brain that plans" or the superior conscious-ness that counterbalances "the hands that build" (destroying first), that is, the revolutionaries.

However, if in *The Fall* and in *Metropolis* the hero undergoes a basic transformation, this process is not so evident regarding Andrés Fava. He seems, at the end of the novel, as self-centered and vague as before. Nor does he seem to have gained a deeper love or understanding of his fellowmen. The internal monologue preceding his entrance into the chateau of Verrières indicates that he joins the revolutionaries because he wants to be near Ludmilla; mankind's sufferings do not appear as the main issue behind his change in attitude (*LM*, pp. 349-56). And yet, even after he joins the Screw Job, Andrés still refuses to adopt a definite stand either in his personal or public life, reiterating his former refusal to renounce one possibility in favor of another (*LM*, pp. 350-51). Fava refuses the limited outlooks of the political activists and the middle class conformists, yet he does not commit himself, either, to the elucidation of a higher reality, as does the Poet in *The Fall*. Lonstein—who says the last words in the novel—seems to stand for such a position, but his utterings are hesitant, half in jest, and do not carry any definite statement of weight.

The ending of the novel is, still, as vague as Cortázar's previous ones, in spite of the significant step it represents by enacting a stage of atonement with the father, after overcoming the dread of the confrontation with Woman/Death. Andrés Fava performs the last action in the novel: he glues a clipping into Manuel's book. But this is a clipping about Lonstein talking to a cadaver in the morgue. Even if Andrés is the main character in the novel, Lonstein-Poe has the final word.

Libro de Manuel illustrates, perhaps better than any other novel by Cortázar, the unique manner in which this author agglutinates in his works a number of heterogeneous elements, where the influences of Keats and Poe play a prominent role, interpenetrating one another. But even when presenting situations that outwardly recall Keatsian themes and structures, the spirit Cortázar interjects into them is, basically, akin to Poe's.

Conclusions

> *. . . This integration of chaos, however, is not possible in any single act or constellation; the individuation it requires is a process of growth embracing the transformations of a whole lifetime; during such a process each individual's capacity for resolving conflict is repeatedly strained to the utmost. This perhaps is why the careers of the great artists of our time are all, in greater or lesser degrees, calvaries. The task of integration facing the great artist today can no longer be performed in a single work, but more than ever before requires a unity of life and work. . . .*

> Erich Neumann, "Art and Time,"
> *Art and the Creative Unconscious*

When I started the present study, I intended to show how the early influences of John Keats and Edgar Allan Poe during the formative period of Cortázar's career had played a central role in shaping the intrinsic duality of the author's outlook, characterized by the opposition between a strongly vitalistic impulse, partially shaped by his studies of Keats, and an equally strong necrophiliac tendency, manifested in his life-long interest in the works of Poe and his disciples. My original hypothesis was that through a process of development lasting the whole length of his career, the author finally achieved a conjunction between these two equivalent forces in his latest novel, *Libro de Manuel*. In this novel, Cortázar returned to the protagonist of his first novel, Andrés Fava, and to the obsessive preoccupation with death which had occupied that character's thoughts throughout the final section of *El examen*. The cycle of the author's development, then, appeared to have been completed with his last novel. In the course of my analysis, however, it gradually became apparent that the cycle is actually closer to an uroboric round, and that the two heterogeneous major influences—Keats and Poe—in Cortázar's works were never equally important.

The influence of Edgar Allan Poe surpasses, by far, that of Keats. Poe was the first major author to shape Cortázar's sensitivity from the time when he was still a child; and Poe continued to be a point of reference to which the author returned throughout the years. The fatherless, lonely, painfully shy, and, at the same time, excessively tender child found a kindred figure in the man who had created the heroes of "The Black Cat," "Eleonora," and "The Fall of the House of Usher," wishing to imitate (by writing his first poems and stories, when he was still a child of eight or nine, in the manner of Poe) the "model" or mentor he had otherwise lacked in real life. Years later, "in "Del sentimiento de no estar del todo" (*VDOM*), Cortázar would still refer to his own childhood by quoting verses from Poe's "Alone."

The developing author found much more to assimilate in the favorite author of his childhood: a detailed body of theoretical essays on the art of the poem and of the short story. Cortázar's own theoretical articles, particularly "Algunos aspectos del cuento" and "Del cuento breve y sus alrededores" but also "Para una poética," in a more surreptitious manner, demonstrate how thoroughly and how faithfully Cortázar learned those first lessons under the guidance of Edgar Allan Poe. The stories in *Bestiario* and *Final del juego* display the economy of words, the carefully manipulated increase of tension through-out the story, the ability to suggest the feeling of horror from the very first sentence, the controlled and "rational" narrative technique that gradually accumulates tension until it explodes in the paroxysm of the character's madness and disintegration: these are the marks of Poe. The themes favored in Cortázar's earliest stories were, likewise, those of Poe: the monologue of the isolated madman, the fear of the returning "double," the supernatural and "terrible" projection of woman; in short, they dealt with *psychological*, rather than supernatural, horror. Hence Poe's ability to imbue the very surroundings of the protagonist and the whole atmosphere of the story with the essence of the horror emanating from the hero's mind became, as well, one of Cortázar's distinctive qualities; the house, the engulfing waters, the isolated ship or island, the awesome descent to the nether world, and the ghostly return of the loved and dreaded "other" became the axes around which Cortázar's early stories revolved.

In Cortázar's works, as in Poe's, woman basically appears as the archetypal Terrible Mother: the superhuman, rending, and absorbing presence that, under the form of the *revenant*, provokes the hero's destruction. However, the human presentation of the archetype in his early works is overshadowed by its non-human manifestations; the Feminine is presented in Cortázar's early works, as well as in Poe's, as the house, the labyrinth, or the stern of the ship, the engulf-ing waters, the initiatic cave, or the "dismembering" animal—the dog. In this respect, *The Narrative of Arthur Gordon Pym*, with its elaborate and cohesive symbolic scheme of reiterative emphasis in order to achieve one central effect, becomes an important influence in the development of Cortázar's stifling atmospheres, suggestive of the Terrible Mother. Just as the whole world of Tsalal is presented as one enormous body, the body of the White Figure, so the whole city in *El examen* becomes symbolic of the overpowering presence of

"Ella" and, in the end, of Ella's most horrible manifestation: Death. The presence of the Terrible Mother as Goddess of Death and Mistress of the Dead recurs in la Maga's apparition in the morgue (in *Rayuela*), in Hélène's desire to stifle life (in *62*), and in the scene of Francine's rape by Andrés while facing the cemetery (in *Libro de Manuel*).

Cortázar's apparent desire to identify with Keats and penetrate his world seems to have responded to a desire to compensate for the nocturnal tendencies he discovered in his own personality. Cortázar was plagued by various phobias, manias, and obsessions at the time when he first centered his attention on Keats. Moreover, it was also at this time that Cortázar first abandoned his mother's home in order to teach in Mendoza province. Later, he started to write the book on Keats just as he had moved into his first apartment in Buenos Aires, in 1948. He seems to have been impelled by a strong desire to *be* like Keats. He found in Keats's poetry that idealization of the state of innocence as a privileged and quasi-divine state that he had also admired in the works of Rilke and Hölderlin, but which was best expressed in the recurrent motif of the Keatsian idyllic "bower."

El examen, written simultaneously with the first part of *Imagen de John Keats*, reflects Keats's influence only in one or two flashbacks where Clara and Andrés return to the idyllic bower of sensation and remember a snail (an allusion to Keats's "snailhorn perception") stretching its horns towards the sun (*E*, p. 81). In view of this, Poe's influence on the novel's structure and themes appears overwhelming. A similar phenomenon is observed in *Bestiario* and *Final del juego*, the two collections that included the stories written from 1948 to 1956.

Keats's influence, nonetheless, was an important factor in defining Cortázar's mythopoetic vision. Cortázar, who had manifested a vivid interest in the study of Jungian concepts, saw in Keats's works a privileged territory for the study of a number of themes that deeply concerned him. Identifying with Keats's difficulty in dealing with "real" women and with the misogynist feelings displayed by Keats at certain periods in his life, he found, in the study of Keats's presentation of the archetypal manifestations of the Feminine, a way of dealing with his own anxieties facing women while keeping them at a distance. Jungian psychology, with its emphasis on the identity of dreams, fantasies, and myth in presenting the structure of the psyche, afforded Cortázar an attractive methodology both for exploring his own anxieties facing the archetype and for presenting it in his fictional works. Keats's works became a model for the mythic projection of the Feminine and a record of the way in which Keats had confronted a problem that Cortázar saw as his own as well. However, Cortázar's study centers only on the manifestations of the "negative" aspects of the archetype of the Magna Mater in Keats's world and neglects other aspects. In Circe, Cortázar sees the basic constellation of the Feminine in Keats's unconscious and the seeds for the later "Belle Dame" and *Lamia*.

The archetypal conception of women, in its turn, became a recurrent phenomenon in Cortázar's works. However, in his hands, the archetypes became far more terrible and destructive than they had ever been in Keats's.

Cortázar's interest in myth and Jungian psychology seems to have been responsible, as well, for the refinement of the author's sensitivity toward quest patterns and structures in the works of Keats and Poe. While the basic quest pattern is universal and can be found under varying forms in all bodies of myth and folklore, the patterns presented in Cortázar's first novels display a strong likeness to those presented in Poe's naval stories, and especially in *Pym*. The concept of the "negative" quest (the symbolic voyage towards a final illumination that ends in madness and dissolution, rather than harmony and fulfillment) was developed by several early Romantics but reached its most influential manifestations in Poe's sea stories, which inspired both Rimbaud's "Le Bateau ivre" and Baudelaire's "Le Voyage," and eventually pervaded the works of many of the later Symbolists and Decadents. *Rayuela* presents a number of parallels with Poe's narrative. Oliveira's quest, however, is no longer inspired, like Pym's, by the purely irrational forces that drove Pym to descend into the cave of the White Figure, seized by an irresistible longing to "fall." Oliveira's is an intellectualized, deliberate, and conscious experimentation with the irrational and the abnormal as a gate to that other reality for which he longs. Yet, while Pym's plunge into uncharted areas of the self represented a true voyage of "discovery," Oliveira's very learning, his acquaintance with the tradition of the negative quest, and his mental review of negative quests in the midst of the very experience, robs it of its liberating or climactic power.

Cortázar attempted to re-create in his latest novel, *Libro de Manuel*, the theme of initiation into the concerns of mankind Keats had developed in the two versions of *Hyperion*. Consciously or not, in the dream of the Cuban he reproduces the major stages in Keats's *The Fall of Hyperion: A Dream*, a work which had presented the Poet's initiation into the concerns of his social group. In Cortázar's novel, however, the dream is modified by a number of elements which differentiate it from the dream in *The Fall*. The "Fritz Lang dream" becomes another manifestation of the central conflict behind the climactic episodes in Cortázar's previous novels: the fear of Death and a paralyzing dread of Woman.

Summing up, then, we have seen, in the course of this study, that Cortázar's attraction to Keats responded to the poet's idealization of the state of innocence and the predominance of "sensation," "instinct," and "feeling" over "reason" and "method" in his early poetics. Cortázar's identification with Poe, on the other hand, arose from his perception of traumas in Poe's life which found a recurrent and overall manifestation in Poe's presentation of the Terrible Mother as Death, with its personal and transpersonal implications. A further link uniting Cortázar to Keats and Poe pertains to the crucial role played by the collective unconscious in their works; for all three, the personal "family drama" opened a window through which the writers communicated with the eternal elements of the collective psyche. By means of this transpersonal projection, the works of these writers presented, symbolically, not only their personal conflicts but the conflicts of their times as well. Thus, when Cortázar attempts to achieve a conjunction between a life and a death instinct, it is not only his personal conflicts he symbolically presents but also the schisms and chaos of our times.

Blackness, *nigredo*, the reign of the Terrible Mother--which, according to depth psychology, typifies our times—means the breakdown of distinctions and forms, and with it, the destruction and decay of all that was known and certain. The interest of the artist, in response to this state, shifts from the human form and the system of consciousness to extrahuman and prehuman forms, to the vitality of the unconscious and the creative forces in the psyche; the human becomes demonic, while the inanimate and animal worlds become human. By plunging into the world of chaos and dissolution and consciously presenting it in his works, the modern artist searches for new symbols for his times in the eternal archetypes of the unconscious. If our world is menaced by chaos, the only way our artists can voice our times is by plunging into that chaos and trying to give it form. In *Rayuela*, Cortázar follows the negative tradition established in Poe's antiquests to express his hero's plunge into the world of chaos; and there, in the midst of the kingdom of death, his hero is visited by the vision of la Maga, the central symbolic figure in the novel. La Maga becomes, for the hero, a ray of hope in the midst of darkness, a synthesis of the natural and the ideal. But here the author's personal conflict blocks his confrontation of the symbol that has arisen in his unconscious and prevents him from fathoming its implications.

The unsolved central problems in *Rayuela* are carried over to the author's subsequent novels, where a peculiar split in the author's aims is discernible as his conscious aims become undermined by the recurrence of that conflict which had remained unsolved. In *Libro de Manuel*, the symbolic initiation into the problems of mankind is overshadowed by the personal symbolism in Andrés' dreams; in them, we find a dramatization of the author's personal problem: the hatred of the Father and the dread of the Mother. In this novel, we find a symbolic solution to this conflict: Woman-Death is defeated, the hero becomes reconciled with the Father figure. Accordingly, the author's originally intended eulogy of the revolutionary groups actually becomes a veiled attack against the excesses of the revolutionaries; for the atonement with the Father neutralizes the unconscious need to attack "the institution" he symbolically represents. The child Manuel, then, represents not only the man of the future, but also the symbolic child born of the conjunction between the opposing forces in the personality, represented by the Mother (instinct) and the Father (reason). However, this process takes place at a purely unconscious level, and the author's repeated refusal to analyze the symbols arising from his unconscious undermines the harmony the conjunction would bring about. Hence, his subsequent works are still "split": the tales in *Octaedro* return to an obsessive preoccupation with death, madness, and the figure of the Terrible Mother. Yet, *Fantomas contra los vampiros multinacionales* displays a light, optimistic tone unusual in the author, and in it he returns—perhaps too consciously—to the figure of the Divine Child already presented in *Libro de Manuel*. Now he presents the forces of oppression as "the vampires" (a recurrent symbol in his earlier works) and the principle of light and hope in an anonymous child (also a predominant symbol in his works). The child, no longer "killed" or otherwise suppressed, closes the story:

> El narrador vio que Fantomas, de pie en el tejado de la casa de enfrente, miraba también al niño. Con un perfecto vuelo de paloma bajó a su lado, buscó en sus bolsillos y sacó un caramelo. El niño lo miró, aceptó el caramelo como la cosa más natural, e hizo un gesto de amistad. Fantomas se elevó en línea recta y se perdió entre las chimeneas.
>
> El niño siguió jugando, y el narrador vio que el sol de la mañana caía sobre su pelo rubio. (*FCVM*, p. 67)

Which of these two works speaks with the author's true, deeper voice? Their very heterogeneity indicates that no conjunction has yet taken place.

Erich Neumann observes that, for the modern writer, integration can no longer be achieved in a single work, but requires, more than ever before, a unity of life and work. The line of development drawn by Cortázar's works points to an integration that has not yet occurred. A final judgement, then, may have to await the course of the author's future creations.

Notes

Foreword

[1] See my "Camaleonismo y vampirismo: la poética de Julio Cortázar," *Revista Ibero-americana*, 45, No. 108-09 (July-Dec. 1979), 475-92.

Introduction

[1] Hernández, "Camaleonismo y vampirismo," pp. 476-85.

[2] Julio Cortázar, "Para una poética," *La Torre*, 2, No. 7 (1954), 130.

[3] Carl Gustav Jung, "On the Relation of Analytical Psychology to Poetry," in *The Spirit in Man, Art and Literature*, trans. R. F. C. Hull, Vol. XV of *The Collected Works of C. G. Jung*, Bollingen Series XX (Princeton: Princeton University Press, 1971), p. 82.

[4] Jorge B. Rivera, "Lo arquetípico en la narrativa argentina del 40," *Nueva novela latinoamericana*, comp. J. Lafforgue, II (Buenos Aires: Paidós, 1974), 174-75.

[5] Graciela de Sola, *Proyecciones del surrealismo en la literatura argentina* (Buenos Aires: Ediciones Culturales Argentinas, 1967), pp. 56-85.

[6] See Julio Cortázar, "Leopoldo Marechal: *Adán Buenosayres,*" *Realidad*, 5, No. 14 (Mar.-Apr. 1949), 232-38.

[7] René Guénon, *Le Règne de la quantité et les signes des temps* (Paris: Gallimard, 1970). For an analysis of quest patterns in *Adán Buenosayres,* see "Pruebas y hazañas de Adán Buenosayres," in *Nueva novela latinoamericana*, comp. J. Lafforgue, II (Buenos Aires: Paidós, 1974), 89-139.

[8] Ernesto B. Rodríguez, *Isla de Pascua* (1940) and *Poemas del origen* (1947); Osvaldo Svanascini, *Este misterio transmutado* (1952) and *Ritual para los días impares* (1959). In Sola, p. 79.

[9] Jorge Luis Borges, *Otras inquisiciones* (Buenos Aires: Emecé, 1966), pp. 72, 94. The lectures were delivered around 1950.

[10] Hernández, "Camaleonismo y vampirismo," pp. 475-86.

11 Interview with Julio Cortázar, 21-22 June 1972.

12 Cf. Burton Feldman and Robert D. Richardson, *The Rise of Modern Mythology, 1680-1860* (Bloomington: Indiana University Press, 1972), pp. 396-99.

13 Hernández, "Camaleonismo y vampirismo," pp. 485-92.

14 Erich Neumann, *The Great Mother: An Analysis of the Archetype*, trans. Ralph Manheim, Bollingen Series XLVII, 2nd ed. (Princeton: Princeton University Press, 1972). Hereafter referred to as *GM*.

15 Jolande Jacobi, *Complex/Archetype/Symbol in the Psychology of C. G. Jung*, trans. Ralph Manheim, Bollingen Series LVII (Princeton: Princeton University Press, 1972), pp. 53, 119-20. For a practical application of this concept, see Erich Neumann, "Leonardo da Vinci and the Mother Archetype," in *Art and the Creative Unconscious*, trans. Ralph Manheim, Bollingen Series LXI, 2nd ed. (Princeton: Princeton University Press, 1972), pp. 3-80.

Chapter 1: Woman as Circe the Magician

1 *IJK*, pp. 266-70.

2 Walter Evert, *Aesthetic and Myth in the Poetry of Keats* (Princeton: Princeton University Press, 1965), p. 91.

3 Evert, p. 91.

4 Robert Graves, *The White Goddess* (New York: Macmillan, 1972), pp. 427-33.

5 Aileen Ward, *John Keats: The Making of a Poet* (New York: Compass-Viking, 1967), pp. 312-13; Robert Gittings, *John Keats* (Boston: Atlantic-Little, Brown, 1968), pp. 358-61.

6 Allen Tate, "A Reading of Keats," *The American Scholar*, 15 (Winter-Spring 1945-46), 62.

7 Rollins, I, 341.

8 Rollins, I, 392.

9 In *Keats and Shakespeare* (London: Oxford University Press, 1926), John Middleton Murry had stated that "Fanny Brawne killed Keats," although he later recanted his idea in *The Mystery of Keats* (see Bibliography). Both works were included in Cortázar's bibliography for *IJK*; but he seems to have stuck to Murry's earlier belief.

10 Rollins, I, 391-92, 394-96; "As a Man in the world I love the rich talk of a Charmian; as an eternal being I love the thought of you [Georgiana Keats]. I should like her to ruin me, and I should like you to save me . . ." (p. 396).

11 Rollins, II, 223-24. The letter of 19 October 1819 expresses a similar feeling: "I must impose chains upon myself–I shall be able to do nothing–I shold [sic] like to cast

the die for love or death—I have no Patience with anything else—if you ever intend to be cruel to me as you say in jest now but perhaps may sometimes be in earnest be so now—and I will—my mind is in a tremble, I cannot tell what I am writing" (p. 224).

[12] Rollins, II, 133.

[13] Luis Harss and Barbara Dohmann, *Into the Mainstream* (New York: Harper & Row, 1967), pp. 214-15.

[14] Letter received from Julio Cortázar, 19 July 1974.

[15] Hernández, "Camaleonismo y vampirismo."

[16] Emma Jung and Marie Louise von Franz, *The Grail Legend*, trans. Andrea Dykes (New York: G. P. Putnam's Sons for the C. G. Jung Foundation for Analytical Psychology, 1970), pp. 40, 43-44.

[17] See, for instance, Cortázar's own account of the critics' reaction to *IJK* (*VDOM*, p. 209). As for Keats, the negative reception of *Endymion* has become legendary.

[18] For a discussion of Keats's annotations on the margins of the *Anatomy*, see Gittings, *John Keats*, pp. 323-24, 345, and Ward, pp. 312-13.

[19] Rollins, I, 395.

[20] Rollins, I, 395.

[21] In Joanna Richardson, *Fanny Brawne* (London: Thames & Hudson, 1952), pp. 20, 172, and Gittings, *John Keats: The Living Year* (New York: Barnes & Noble, 1968), pp. 3-33, 59-60, 230-35 (this is the sole reference to this Gittings work).

[22] Walter Jackson Bate, *John Keats* (New York: Oxford University Press, 1966), pp. 167-68; Ward, pp. 121-22; Gittings, *John Keats*, pp. 139-40; Murry, *Keats* (New York: Minerva Press, 1968), p. 123. These critics speculate about such a possibility.

[23] Rollins, I, 403-04.

[24] None of Keats's later critics has been so totally negative when interpreting the Fanny Brawne affair. See, for instance, Murry, *Keats*, pp. 19-81; Ward, pp. 292-324; Gittings, *John Keats*, pp. 327-30.

[25] Rollins, II, 126.

[26] "Medicines as well as poisons are numinous contents that have been acquired and communicated in mysterious wise. The communicators and administrators of this aspect of the Feminine—originally almost always women—are sacral figures, i.e., priestesses" (*GM*, p. 60).

[27] Freudian psychology generally establishes a connection between the eyes and the male genitalia. Thus, Oedipus' self-blinding is seen as punitive castration. In Ancient Greece, the interpreters of the oracle of Themis were blinded and had been castrated in

honor of the goddess; in this case, blindness appears as a symbolic surrendering of the male realm, that of "visionary reason," in favor of the feminine realm, that of "blind intuition." Also, see note 28 below.

28 "For a boy to be really successful, it might be wise to castrate him; for Byzantium was the eunuch's paradise. Even the noblest parents were not above mutilating their sons to help their advancement. . . . A large proportion of the Patriarchs of Constantinople were eunuchs; and eunuchs were particularly encouraged in the Civil Service, where the castrated bearer of a title took precedence of his unmutilated compeer and where many high ranks were reserved for eunuchs alone"–Steven Runciman, *Byzantine Civilization* (New York: Meridian, 1956), pp. 162-63.

29 Erich Neumann, *The Origins and History of Consciousness*, trans. R. F. C. Hull, Bollingen Series XLII (Princeton: Princeton University Press, 1971; first ed. 1949), p. 58.

30 Gittings, *John Keats*, p. 303.

31 Gittings, *John Keats*, p. 303.

32 "The symbol inherently contains the repulsive element, but keeps it at a distance, so that he [Keats] does not have to face it in terms of a common experience, his own. . . . " (Tate, p. 62).

33 Cf. Murry, *Keats*, p. 237; Gittings, *John Keats*, pp. 338-41.

34 Gittings, *John Keats*, p. 301: "Keats was living out the diversities of love which had formed part of his satisfaction with his treatment of *Lamia*, a love which included every possible element"; Morris Dickstein, *Keats and His Poetry* (Chicago: University of Chicago Press, 1971): "Love, possession and sadistic desire for domination intermingle here, under the significant banner of Keats's old ideal of 'luxury' "; Murry, *Keats,* p. 237: " 'Light and shade,' 'pro and con,' are in Keats's experience the very law and principle of life–and death."

35 Murry, *Keats*, p. 231.

36 J. E. Cirlot, *A Dictionary of Symbols*, trans. Jack Sage (New York: Philosophical Library, 1962), pp. 127-28.

37 M. Esther Harding, *Woman's Mysteries, Ancient and Modern*, 2nd ed. (New York: G. P. Putnam's Sons for the C. G. Jung Foundation for Analytical Psychology, 1971; first ed. 1935), pp. 103-04.

38 Cortázar has observed as follows:

El capítulo del "anima" es muy hermoso, y creo que tienes toda la razón al ver así a la Maga. Eres la primera en asimilarla a esta concepción de Jung, y creo que tu interpretación echa por tierra muchas otras que andan por ahí. Ahí sí entro de lleno en tu campo, sin el menor esfuerzo; porque yo mismo siento, retrospectivamente, las fuerzas que me impulsaron y me compulsaron cuando escribí ese libro; no tenían nombres ni parámetros psicoanalíticos, pero yo las sentía, desde el tablón inicial (y bien que lo citas) hasta el final del libro. Sólo en algunos momentos de

62 he vivido tan sometido a esas potencias que tiran y empujan desde abajo, si abajo quiere decir alguna cosa. Y a propósito de *62*, me deslumbró que vieras en Hélène un complemento de la Maga; eso me aclara muchas cosas, mi fascinación personal por Hélène, vagamente basada en una mujer que sólo vi dos o tres veces y a quien hubiera querido conocer íntimamente: lesbiana (no tengo pruebas), misteriosa, esquiva, cruel, bella, distante, y a la vez irradiando una atracción permamente: de ahí nació Hélène, y es cierto que es la otra mitad, por decirlo así, de la Maga. (Letter received from Julio Cortázar, written at Saignon, 30 June 1973.)

39 C. G. Jung, *Symbols of Transformation,* trans. R. F. C. Hull, 2nd ed. Vol. V of *The Collected Works of C. G. Jung,* Bollingen Series XX (Princeton: Princeton University Press, 1970), p. 370.

40 Jung, *Symbols of Transformation,* p. 369.

Chapter 2: Woman as Death

1 This information was obtained from a footnote on p. 95 of Hervey Allen's *Israfel: The Life and Times of Edgar Allan Poe* (New York: Farrar & Rinehart, 1934). It is significant that Cortázar saw fit to include such an assertion, absent from other biographies of Poe.

2 Cf. Mario Praz, *The Romantic Agony* (London: Oxford University Press, 1970; first ed. 1930), pp. 201, et passim.

3 Arthur Hobson Quinn, *Edgar Allan Poe* (New York: Appleton, Century, Crofts, 1941), p. 86.

4 William Bittner, *Poe: A Biography* (Boston: Atlantic-Little, Brown, 1962), p. 35.

5 According to Allen, Poe was raving about Mrs. Whitman even before he met her; he sarcastically concludes that "Apparently, he was as much in love with her *then* as he ever was" (Allen, p. 607). In "The Raven" and in a story, he had referred to Virginia Clemm with names that were actually variations of the magic name "Helen": "Eleanora" and "Lenore."

6 In Bittner, p. 248.

7 When interpreting Poe's marriage to Virginia as an attempt to protect himself with her "pure love" from more demanding relationships with other women, Cortázar faithfully follows the lead of Allen's argument. Allen claims that "the man [Poe] was so nervously and complexly organized that the strong emotions of sex, the most profound and disturbing in the world, threatened not only to make all creative work impossible but literally to drive him insane. The anticipation was more than he could bear: the realization of it, after Virginia's death at Fordham, confirmed his fears" (Allen, p. 458).

8 Montagu Slater, *The Centenary Poe*, in Bittner, p. 276.

9 Original Autograph MS, Poe to Mrs. Whitman, 1 October 1848, Collection of J. K. Lilly, Jr., in Quinn, pp. 575-76.

10 Allen, however, understates Helen's importance, claiming he really loved Mrs. Richmond but wished to marry Helen for convenience (Allen, pp. 601-29). In this respect, Cortázar's attitude is closer to Quinn's (pp. 572-92).

11 Quinn points out the resemblance between certain letters to "Annie" and those to Virginia (Quinn, p. 592).

12 According to Bittner (pp. 242-43) and Allen (p. 621), Poe actually attempted suicide in order to make "Annie," the true object of his love, come to him.

13 Allen, pp. 620-21; Quinn, pp. 590-92.

14 *Complete Works*, III, 273.

15 *Complete Works*, II, 260-61.

16 *Complete Works*, II, 13.

17 Richard Wilbur, who has studied the theme of the house in Poe's works, observes that "circumscription, in Poe's tales, means the exclusion from consciousness of the so-called real world, the world of time and reason and physical fact; it means the isolation of the poetic soul in visionary reverie or trance. When we find one of Poe's characters in a remote valley or claustral room, we know that he is in the process of dreaming himself out of the world"—"The House of Poe," in *Poe: A Collection of Critical Essays,* ed. Robert Regan (Englewood Cliffs, N. J.: Prentice-Hall, 1967), p. 104.

18 *Complete Works*, III, 281.

19 Jacobi, pp. 90-92.

20 *Complete Works*, III, 275.

21 *Complete Works*, III, 280-81.

22 *Complete Works*, III, 277-78.

23 *Complete Works*, III, 274.

24 Once more, we observe Cortázar's peculiar use of animal symbolism to objectify the protagonists' psychological fears; the frogs that bark like dogs resemble the rabbits in "Carta," which "gritaban, gritaban como yo no creo que griten los conejos" (*B*, p. 33). Like the rabbits and "el perro," the frogs foretell the hero's doom.

25 *Complete Works*, III, 276.

26 Cortázar observes regarding this story:

En este cuento (uno de mis primeros, por cierto, parcialmente reescrito años después pero sin ningún cambio básico) la clave es la relación homosexual entre el narrador y Lucio. Como jamás aludes a ella, porque acaso no te interesa para tu análisis, te la señalo de todos modos. Esquemáticamente, mi hilo narrativo se basó en esta secuencia: El narrador siente que va a perder a Lucio. El narrador sueña el sueño del ahogado. Cuando invita a pasear a Lucio por la isla, los dos saben que algo va a suceder entre ellos. Cuando Lucio lo acusa de haberle robado su sueño, y el narrador "ve" el final, es decir, se ve a sí mismo ahogado, comprende que Lucio ha pensado en matarlo, que lo está pensando más que nunca ahora que de alguna manera ha sido descubierto. Entonces el narrador mata a Lucio, cambia un ahogado por otro. Pero Lucio empieza a "volver", y son las referencias finales a esa "vuelta" espectral que permiten deducir cualquier cosa: lo directamente fantástico, o sea, que alguna noche Lucio ahogará al narrador, o bien que este se suicidará para cumplir el sueño de Lucio que él había soñado." (Letter received from Cortázar, written at Saignon, 30 June 1973.)

[27] Cf. Ana María Hernández, "Vampires and Vampiresses: A Reading of *62*," *Books Abroad,* 50, No. 3 (Summer 1976), 573.

[28] *Complete Works,* III, 296.

[29] In Sidney Kaplan, "An Introduction to *Pym*," in *Poe: A Collection of Critical Essays,* ed. Robert Regan (Englewood Cliffs, N. J.: Prentice-Hall, 1967), p. 146.

[30] Bittner, p. 90.

[31] Floyd Stovall, *"The Narrative of Arthur Gordon Pym* by Edgar Allan Poe, with an introduction by Richard Wilbur (Boston: David R. Godine, 1973)," in *The Poe Messenger,* 5, No. 1 (Fall 1974), 6; Kaplan, p. 151; Bittner, pp. 121-22.

[32] Bittner, p. 132.

[33] Poe's acquaintance with Anthon, however, was prior to his second sojourn in New York; they had corresponded in 1836 while Poe was in Richmond. In the Preface to his Dictionary (New York: Harper & Brothers, 1875; first ed. 1841), Anthon declares that his work is not just an improved edition of Lempriere's, but "a work entirely new, and resembling its predecessor in nothing but the name. . . ." He declares that his intention has been "to lay before the student the most important speculations of the two schools (the Mystic and the anti-Mystic) which now divide the learned of Europe . . . it has been the aim of the author to give a fair and impartial view of both systems, although he cannot doubt but that the former will appear to the student by far the more attractive of the two" (p. vii). Most of Anthon's information proceeded from his vast collection of treatises by the syncretists, whose titles he lists at the beginning of the Dictionary. Among them, we find J. Bryant's *A New System of Mythology,* 6 vols. (London, 1807), Court de Gebelin's *Monde primitif,* 9 vols. (Paris, 1787), and G. S. Faber's *Origin of Pagan Idolatry,* 3 vols. (London, 1816).

[34] Anthon to Poe, New York, 1 June 1837. In Allen, p. 339.

[35] Bittner, p. 131.

[36] *Pinakidia, Complete Works,* XIV, 52, 53 (this fragment later appeared incorporated into the text of "The Purloined Letter," VI, 45), 113; *Eureka,* XVI, 217.

[37] Killis Campbell, *The Mind of Poe* (New York: Russell & Russell, 1962; first pub. 1933), p. 180.

38 All quotations from *The Narrative of Arthur Gordon Pym* refer to *The Works of Edgar Allan Poe*, 4 vols. (New York: A. C. Armstrong & Son, 1884), Vol. IV; hereafter referred to as *Pym*. This text conforms to that of the Virginia edition.

39 Kaplan, p. 155.

40 Poe referred to one of these treatises when he remarked about Emerson: "Albert, in his Hebrew Dictionary, pretends to discover in each word, in its root, in its letters, and in the manner of pronouncing them, the reason of its significance. Leescher in his treatise *De causiis Linguae Hebrae* carries the matter even farther" (*Pinakidia, Complete Works*, XIV, 70).

41 Kaplan, pp. 155-56.

42 In Feldman and Richardson, pp. 247-48.

43 In Feldman and Richardson, p. 400.

44 Feldman and Richardson, p. 405.

45 Graves, p. 372.

46 " 'Anadyomene': a celebrated picture of Venus, painted by Apelles, which originally adorned the temple of Aesculapius at Cos. It represented the goddess *rising out of the sea* . . ." (Anthon, p. 130; his italics). " 'Anaitis': a goddess of Armenia, who appears to be the same with the Venus of the western nations. She is identical also with the goddess of Nature, worshipped among the Persians. (Creuzer, *Symbolik*, vol. 2, p. 27)." Anthon proceeds to relate this goddess with the Persian Anahid ("the name of the morning star and of the female genius that directs with her lyre the harmony of the spheres") and with the Asiatic Tanat, at times confounded with Diana and at others with Minerva. He also relates her to the Egyptian Neith (with the article prefixed, A-neith) (Anthon, p. 131).
    Under "Anna," we find: ". . . a goddess, in whose honour the Romans instituted a festival. She was, according to the common account, Anna, the daughter of Belus, and sister of Dido. . . ." Many legends about Anna Perenna, Anthon proceeds, were associated with her festival, which took place around March 15 (Pym descends into the cave on March 22). Anna Perenna was the moon goddess, in addition to the earth goddess: "Anna Perenna is called the moon . . . , and it is she that conducts the moons her sisters, and who at the same time directs and governs the humid sphere: thus she reposes forever in the river Numicius, and runs on for ever with it. She is the course of the moons, of the years, of time in general. . . ." Finally, the author identifies her with the Anna Pourna Devi of the Hindus (Anthon, pp. 137-38).

47 "Ovid and Virgil knew their Goddess Anna Perenna to have been a sister of Belus, or Bel, who was a masculinization of the Sumerian Goddess Belili" (Graves, p. 371).

48 Harding, pp. 160-61.

49 I found no entry for "Belili," "Ishtar," or "Kilili" in Anthon's; however, the article on "Astarte" of Syria (identical with Ishtar of Babylonia) identifies this goddess as Magna

Mater: " 'Astarte,' observes R. P. Knight, 'was precisely the same as Cybele, or universal mother of the Phrygians. She was . . . by some called Juno, by others Venus, and by others held up to be Nature, or the cause which produced the beginning and seeds of things from Humidity so that she comprehended in one personification both these goddesses who were, accordingly, sometimes blended in one symbolical figure by the very ancient Greek artists. Her statue at Hierapolis was variously composed so as to signify many attributes, like those of the Ephesian Diana, Berecynthian Mother, and others of the kind. It was placed in the interior part of the temple, accessible only to priests of the higher order . . .' " (Anthon, p. 218). In a fragment of *Pinakidia*, Poe refers to the temple of Belus—male counterpart of Belili (*Complete Works*, XIV, 65).

[50] Carl Gustav Jung, *The Archetypes and the Collective Unconscious*, trans. R. F. C. Hull, 2nd ed., Vol. IX of *The Collected Works of C. G. Jung*, Bollingen Series XX (Princeton: Princeton University Press, 1971), p. 71.

[51] Jung, *The Archetypes*, p. 200. Further references to Rider Haggard's novel occur in pp. 28, 30, 285, and 286, and in *Symbols of Transformation*, p. 437.

[52] "Haghesa," the name of the white goddess in "El ídolo de las Cícladas," also seems to derive from She's real name, Ayesha.

[53] Herbert Silberer, *Hidden Symbolism of Alchemy and the Occult Arts*, trans. Smith Ely Jeliffe (New York: Dover, 1971; first pub. 1917), p. 123.

[54] "Rebirth" must be preceded by "death"; Andrés Fava cannot withstand the idea of death.

[55] Letter received from Julio Cortázar, 19 July 1974.

[56] Otto Rank, *The Double*, trans. Harry Tucker, Jr. (Chapel Hill: University of North Carolina Press, 1971), p. 277.

[57] Mircea Eliade observes in *Myths, Dreams and Mysteries*, trans. Philip Mairet (New York: Torchbooks-Harper & Row, 1967), p. 171:

In prehistoric times the cavern, often resembling or ritually transformed into, a labyrinth, was at once a theatre of initiation and a place where the dead were buried. The labyrinth, in its turn, was homologized with the body of the Earth-Mother. To penetrate into a labyrinth or a cavern was the equivalent of a mystical return to the Mother—an end pursued in the rites of initiation as well as in funeral obsequies. The researches of Jackson Knight have shown us how slow it is to disappear, this symbolism of the labyrinth regarded as the body of a telluric Goddess.

[58] Saúl Sosnowski, *Julio Cortázar: una búsqueda mítica* (Buenos Aires: Noé, 1974), p. 93.

[59] *Complete Works*, II, 267-68.

[60] *Complete Works*, II, 268.

Chapter 3: The Individual Quest

[1] Joseph Campbell, *The Hero With a Thousand Faces,* 2nd ed., Bollingen Series XVII (Princeton: Princeton University Press, 1973), p. 30. Hereafter referred to as *HWTF.* This basic structure of the quest pattern is also pointed out by Jung and von Franz, pp. 9-38; Harding, pp. 216-41; Mircea Eliade, *Rites and Symbols of Initiation,* trans. Willard R. Trask (New York: Harper & Row, 1965), pp. 1-40.

[2] I have used Harding's interpretation of the meaning behind each major stage or "initiation" in the process of spiritual transformation symbolized by the "quest" as a frame of reference (*Woman's Mysteries,* pp. 216-41). Jung and von Franz provide an analogous interpretation in *The Grail Legend.*

[3] Cirlot, p. 36.

[4] Cirlot, p. 36.

[5] "En general, éstos [los críticos] han transitado en sus explicaciones, por comodidad o desorientación, el mismo camino que Cortázar les ofrecía. Sin rebasar las categorías puestas en órbita por el narrador, glosando las digresiones sobre su experimento novelesco, los comentaristas han entonado un coro entusiasta, como si formaran un nuevo Club de la Serpiente . . ."–Jaime Concha, "Criticando *Rayuela,*" *Hispamérica,* año IV, anejo I (1975), p. 13.

[6] Concha, p. 13.

[7] Cf. Evelyn Picon-Garfield, *¿Es Julio Cortázar un surrealista?* (Madrid: Gredos, 1975), pp. 109-18; and my article "La mujer como médium," *Zona: carga y descarga,* 2, No. 7 (Sept. 1974), pp. 25-27.

[8] The relationship between the two episodes and the test of "solidarity" is explicit in the text itself. As Oliveira encourages the pianist, he thinks "Le hizo gracia esa especie de solidaridad. . . . De golpe comprobaba que todas sus reacciones derivaban de una cierta simpatía por Berthe Trépat. . . . de golpe se sorprendía con ganas de ir al hospital a visitar al viejo, o aplaudiendo a esa loca encorsetada" (*R,* p. 130).

[9] Regarding these parallels, Cortázar observes:

Donde me dejaste absolutamente sin aliento es . . . cuando haces el esquema comparativo de los capítulos 41 y 52. Que un escritor trabaje sin *saber* lo que está escribiendo y que sólo lo descubra cuando alguien, más lúcido que él, muestra lo que tú has mostrado ahí. . . . Es vertiginoso, tiene algo de horrible y de maravilloso a la vez. Es como la negación de la libertad en el creador. Entonces, ¿todo lo que escribimos está ya decidido desde otras potencias de las que actúan superficialmente mientras escribimos? Trato de acordarme, de pensar en lo que me pasaba por la cabeza mientras escribía *Rayuela;* y no, no era así, no había ningún esquema, ninguna relación prevista entre esos dos capítulos, como tampoco la había en el capítulo del tablón y en el que luego suprimí. . . . ¿*Quién* escribe nuestros libros, Ana María? (Letter received from Julio Cortázar, 5 June 1973.)

[10] Guénon, *Le Règne,* p. 361.

11 Guénon, *Le Règne*, p. 363.

12 Guénon, *Le Règne*, p. 363.

13 Guénon, *Le Règne*, p. 366.

14 Fyodor Dostoievsky, *The Possessed*, trans. C. Garnett, introd. Philip Rahv (Greenwich, Conn.: Fawcett, 1966), p. xviii.

15 Guénon, *Le Règne*, p. 364.

16 Guénon, *Le Règne*, p. 365.

17 "Art and Time," in *Art and the Creative Unconscious*, p. 114.

18 Neumann, "Art and Time," p. 123.

19 And even in his life: "Por mi parte vivo una vida seca y sin encantos, ni siquiera jugar con un gatito; paso de un papel a otro, de una reunión a otra, tengo que leer incontables artículos que me enseñan lo que no sé en materias geopolíticas, y me aburro como una ostra. Qué envidia le tengo a la gente que hace su deber gustándole; yo lo hago con una extraña sensación de estar caminando detrás de mí mismo, lejano y solitario . . ." (Letter received from Julio Cortázar, 21 January 1975).

20 5. When the archetype as such is "touched by consciousness," it can manifest itself either on the "lower," biological plane and take form, for instance, as an expression of instinct or as an instinctual dynamism, or on the "higher," spiritual plane as an image or idea. In the latter case the raw material of imagery and meaning are added to it, and the *symbol* is born. The *symbolic guise* in which it becomes visible varies and changes according to the outward and inward circumstances of the individual and the times. . . .
   6. The symbol acquires a certain degree of autonomy in its confrontation with the conscious mind. [It is at this stage that we find the creation of literary characters that are, so to say, "independent" from the author.]
   7. The meaning with which the symbol is "pregnant" more or less *compels the conscious mind to come to terms with it.* . . . [My italics]
   8. The symbol may
      a) be brought closer to the conscious mind by understanding and be felt and recognized as in some degree belonging to the ego, but without being wholly fathomed, so that it continues to be "alive" and effective; [This phenomenon can be observed throughout Cortázar's writings up to *Rayuela*, when a *confrontation* is attempted.]
      b) be completely fathomed and explored. Then it seems wholly integrated with the ego and assimilated by the conscious mind, but it loses its "life" and efficacy, and becomes a mere allegory, a "sign," or a conceptually unambiguous content of consciousness;
      c) not be understood at all: it may confront the ego consciousness as an expression of a complex hidden, so to speak, behind it, as a hostile foreign body, split off from it and causing a dissociation in the psyche. It then becomes an *autonomous splinter psyche* which can make itself felt in the form of "spirits," "hallucinations," etc. (Jacobi, pp. 120-21)

21 Neumann, "Art and Time," p. 131.

Chapter 4: The Collective Quest

1 Cf. Joaquín Roy, *Julio Cortázar ante su sociedad* (Barcelona: Península, 1974).

2 Rollins, II, 102.

3 Particularly in the letter to Tom Keats of 25-27 June 1818.

4 Ward, p. 221; Gittings, *John Keats,* p. 261, and generally.

5 Jane Harrison, *Themis* (Cambridge: At the University Press, 1912), p. 514.

6 Cf. note 1, Chapter 3.

7 Dorothy van Ghent, "Keats's Myth of the Hero," *Keats-Shelley Journal,* 3 (1954), 12.

8 Dickstein, pp. 248-53; Murry, *Keats,* pp. 238-49.

9 Campbell, *HWTF,* pp. 90-93.

10 Dickstein, p. 260.

11 Dickstein, p. 261.

12 Harding, p. 238.

13 Cirlot, pp. 43-44.

14 Gittings, *John Keats,* p. 346.

15 Yet, by "defeating" a feminine character that no longer possesses the numinous, symbolic power of Claudia, la Maga, or Hélène, the hero is not really confronting the archetypal Terrible Mother and incorporating the meaning in her—Ludmilla and Francine have no longer any transpersonal meaning in the novel. It is now a *father* figure that is endowed with archetypal contents.

16 M. Esther Harding, *The Parental Image: Its Injury and Reconstruction* (New York: G. P. Putnam's Sons for the C. G. Jung Foundation for Analytical Psychology, 1965), p. 148.

17 Harding, *Parental Image,* p. 149.

18 C. G. Jung, *Mysterium Coniunctionis,* trans. R. F. C. Hull, 2nd ed., Vol. XIV of *The Collected Works of C. G. Jung,* Bollingen Series XX (Princeton: Princeton University Press, 1970), p. 182.

19 *Metropolis,* dir. Fritz Lang, Germany, 1926. Based on the novel by Thea von Harbou Lang. Cf. *Janus Films: The Classic Collection* (New York: Janus Films, 1975); Chris Steinbrunner and Burt Goldblatt, *Cinema of the Fantastic* (New York: Gallahad Books, 1972), pp. 15-32.

Bibliography

Allen, Hervey. *Israfel: The Life and Times of Edgar Allan Poe.* New York: Farrar & Rinehart, 1934.

Alterton, Margaret B. *Origins of Poe's Critical Theory.* Iowa City: University of Iowa Press, 1925.

Anthon, Charles. *A Classical Dictionary.* "A classical dictionary containing an account of the principal proper names mentioned in ancient authors and intended to elucidate all the important points connected with the geography, history, biography, mythology, and fine arts of the Greeks and Romans." New York: Harper & Brothers, 1875; first ed. 1841.

Barrenechea, Ana Mar̄ía, "La estructura de *Rayuela* de Julio Cortázar." *Nueva novela latinoamericana.* Comp. J. Lafforgue. II. Buenos Aires: Paidós, 1974, 222-47.

———, and Emma Susana Speratti Piñero. *La literatura fantástica en la Argentina.* México: Fondo de Cultura Económica, 1957.

Bate, Walter Jackson. *John Keats.* New York: Oxford University Press, 1966.

Baudelaire, Charles. *L'Art romantique. Suivi de Fusées, Mon cœur mis à nu et Pauvre Belgique.* Utrecht: Julliard, 1964.

Bierce, Ambrose. *Ghost and Horror Stories.* Selected with an introd. by E. F. Bleiler. New York: Dover, 1964.

Bittner, William. *Poe: A Biography.* Boston: Atlantic-Little, Brown, 1962.

Bodkin, Maud. *Archetypal Patterns in Poetry: Psychological Studies of Imagination.* London: Oxford University Press, 1968; first pub. 1934.

Bonaparte, Marie (Princess). *The Life and Works of Edgar Allan Poe: A Psychoanalytic Interpretation.* Trans. John Rodker. London: Imago, 1949; first pub. in French, 1933.

Borges, Jorge Luis. *Antiguas literaturas germánicas.* México: Fondo de Cultura Económica, 1951.

———. *Otras inquisiciones.* Buenos Aires: Emecé, 1966.

Brooks, Cleanth. *Modern Poetry and the Tradition.* Chapel Hill: University of North Carolina Press, 1939.

Campbell, Joseph. *The Hero With a Thousand Faces.* 2nd ed. Bollingen Series XVII. Princeton: Princeton University Press, 1973; first ed. 1949.

———. *The Masks of God.* 4 vols. New York: Viking, 1972; first pub. 1959.

Campbell, Killis. *The Mind of Poe and Other Studies.* New York: Russell & Russell, 1962; first pub. 1933.

Carlson, Eric W., ed. *The Recognition of Edgar Allan Poe: Selected Criticism Since 1829.* Ann Arbor: University of Michigan Press, 1970.

Cirlot, J. E. *A Dictionary of Symbols.* Trans. Jack Sage. Introd. Herbert Read. New York: Philosophical Library, 1962.

Colvin, Sidney. *Keats.* 1887; rpt. London: Macmillan, 1968.

Concha, Jaime. "Criticando *Rayuela.*" *Hispamérica,* año IV, anejo I (1975), pp. 131-51.

Cortázar, Julio. *LR: Los reyes.* Buenos Aires: Angel Gulab, 1949.

———. *E: El examen.* MS. Buenos Aires, 1950. Kept by Cortázar in Paris.

———. *B: Bestiario.* Buenos Aires: Sudamericana, 1951.

———. *IJK: Imagen de John Keats.* MS. Buenos Aires-Paris, 1952. Kept by Cortázar in Paris.

———. *OP:* Edgar Allan Poe, *Obras en prosa.* Trans. and prologue by Julio Cortázar. Madrid: Revista de Occidente, 1956.

———. *AS: Las armas secretas.* Buenos Aires: Sudamericana, 1958.

———. *P: Los premios.* Buenos Aires: Sudamericana, 1960.

———. *R: Rayuela.* Buenos Aires: Sudamericana, 1963.

———. *F: Final del juego.* 2nd ed. Buenos Aires: Sudamericana, 1964; first ed. México, 1956.

———. *VDOM: La vuelta al día en ochenta mundos.* México: Siglo XXI, 1967.

———. *62: 62: Modelo para armar.* Buenos Aires: Sudamericana, 1968.

———. *UR:Ultimo round.* México: Siglo XXI, 1969.

———. *PM:Pameos y meopas.* Barcelona: Ocnos, 1971.

———. *PO: Prosa del observatorio.* Buenos Aires: Sudamericana, 1972.

Cortázar, Julio. *LM*: *Libro de Manuel*. Buenos Aires: Sudamericana, 1973.

———. *FCVM*: *Fantomas contra los vampiros multinacionales*. México: PEPA, 1975.

———. *O*: *Octaedro*. Buenos Aires: Sudamericana, 1974.

———. "Rimbaud," by Julio Denis. *Huella* (Buenos Aires), No. 2 (1941).

———. "La urna griega en la poesía de Keats." *Revista de Estudios Clásicos* (Universidad de Cuyo), 2, No. 49-61 (1946), 45-91.

———. "Muerte de Antonin Artaud." *Sur*, No. 163 (May 1948), pp. 80-82.

———. "Leopoldo Marechal: *Adán Buenosayres.*" *Realidad*, 5, No. 14 (Mar.-Apr. 1949), 232-38.

———. "Un cadáver viviente." *Realidad*, 5, No. 15 (May-June 1949), 349-50.

———. "François Porché: *Baudelaire, historia de un alma.*" *Sur*, No. 176 (June 1949), pp. 70-74.

———. "Para una poética." *La Torre*, 2, No. 7 (1954), 121-38.

———. "Algunos aspectos del cuento." *Casa de las Américas* (La Habana), No. 15-16 (1962-63), pp. 3-14.

Curutchet, Juan Carlos. *Julio Cortázar o la crítica de la razón pragmática*. Madrid: Nacional, 1972.

Davidson, Edward H. *Poe: A Critical Study*. Cambridge, Mass.: Harvard University Press, 1973.

De Selincourt, Ernest. *John Keats: The Poems*. Oxford: Clarendon Press, 1926.

Dickstein, Morris. *Keats and His Poetry*. Chicago: University of Chicago Press, 1971.

Dostoievsky, Fyodor. *The Possessed*. Trans. C. Garnett. Introd. Philip Rahv. Greenwich, Conn.: Fawcett, 1966.

Eliade, Mircea. *Rites and Symbols of Initiation: The Mysteries of Birth and Rebirth*. Trans. Willard R. Trask. New York: Torchbooks-Harper & Row, 1965. For other editions of this entry and the following entry see Douglas Allen and Dennis Doeing. *Mircea Eliade: An Annotated Bibliography*. New York: Garland, 1980.

———. *Myths, Dreams and Mysteries: The Encounter Between Contemporary Faiths and Archaic Realities*. Trans. Philip Mairet. New York: Torchbooks-Harper & Row, 1967.

Englekirk, John E. *Edgar Allan Poe in Hispanic Literature*. New York: Russell & Russell, 1972; first pub. 1934.

Evert, Walter. *Aesthetic and Myth in the Poetry of Keats*. Princeton: Princeton University Press, 1965.

Fausset, Hugh l'Anson. *Keats: A Study in Development*. Hamden, Conn.: Archon Books, 1966; first pub. 1922.

Feldman, Burton, and Robert D. Richardson. *The Rise of Modern Mythology, 1680-1860*. Bloomington: Indiana University Press, 1972.

Filer, Malva E. *Los mundos de Julio Cortázar*. New York: Las Américas, 1970.

Fromm, Erich. *The Forgotten Language: An Introduction to the Understanding of Dreams, Fairytales and Myths*. New York: Grove Press, 1957; first pub. 1951.

Frye, Northrop. *A Study of English Romanticism*. New York: Random House, 1968.

Fuentes, Carlos. *La nueva novela hispanoamericana*. México: Joaquín Mortiz, 1969.

García-Canclini, Néstor. *Cortázar: una antropología poética*. Buenos Aires: Nova, 1968.

Garrod, H. W. *Keats*. Oxford: Clarendon Press, 1939.

Giacoman, Helmy, ed. *Homenaje a Julio Cortázar*. New York: Las Américas, 1971.

Gittings, Robert. *John Keats: The Living Year, 21 September 1818 to 21 September 1819*. New York: Barnes & Noble, 1968; first ed. 1954.

————. *John Keats*. Boston: Atlantic-Little, Brown, 1968.

Graves, Robert. *The White Goddess*. New York: Macmillan, 1972; first pub. 1946.

Guénon, René. *Le Règne de la quantité et les signes des temps*. Paris: Gallimard, 1970; first pub. 1945.

Guibert, Rita. *Seven Voices: Seven Latin American Writers Talk to Rita Guibert*. New York: Knopf, 1972.

Halliburton, David. *Edgar Allan Poe: A Phenomenological View*. Princeton: Princeton University Press, 1973.

Harding, M. Esther. *Woman's Mysteries, Ancient and Modern: A Psychological Interpretation of the Feminine Principle as Portrayed in Myth, Story, and Dreams*. 2nd ed. New York: G. P. Putnam's Sons for the C. G. Jung Foundation for Analytical Psychology, 1971; first ed. 1935; revised ed. 1955.

————. *The Parental Image: Its Injury and Reconstruction*. New York: G. P. Putnam's Sons for the C. G. Jung Foundation for Analytical Psychology, 1965.

Harrison, Jane Ellen. *Themis: A Study of the Social Origins of Greek Religion*. Cambridge: At the University Press, 1912.

Harrison, Max. *Kings of Jazz: Charlie Parker.* New York: A. S. Barnes, 1961.

Harss, Luis, and Barbara Dohmann. *Into the Mainstream: Conversations with Latin American Writers.* New York: Harper & Row, 1967.

Hernández, Ana María. "Conversación con Julio Cortázar." *Nueva narrativa hispanoamericana,* 3, No. 2 (Sept. 1973), 31-40.

———. "La mujer como médium." *Zona: carga y descarga,* 2, No. 7 (Sept. 1974), 25-27.

———. "Vampires and Vampiresses: A Reading of *62.*" *Books Abroad,* 50, No. 3 (Summer 1976), 570-76.

———. "Camaleonismo y vampirismo: la poética de Julio Cortázar." *Revista Iberoamericana,* 45, No. 108-09 (July-Dec. 1979), 475-92.

Jacobi, Jolande. *Complex/Archetype/Symbol in the Psychology of C. G. Jung.* Trans. Ralph Manheim. Bollingen Series LVII. Princeton: Princeton University Press, 1972; first ed. in English, 1959; in German, 1957.

Janus Films: The Classic Collection. (Descriptive Catalog). New York: Janus Films, 1975.

Jung, Carl Gustav. *Symbols of Transformation.* Trans. R. F. C. Hull. 2nd ed. Vol. V of *The Collected Works of C. G. Jung.* Bollingen Series XX. Princeton: Princeton University Press, 1970.

———. *The Archetypes and the Collective Unconscious.* Trans. R. F. C. Hull. 2nd ed. Vol. IX of *The Collected Works of C. G. Jung.* Bollingen Series XX. Princeton: Princeton University Press, 1971.

———. *Mysterium Coniunctionis.* Trans. R. F. C. Hull. 2nd ed. Vol. XIV of *The Collected Works of C. G. Jung.* Bollingen Series XX. Princeton: Princeton University Press, 1970.

———. *The Spirit in Man, Art and Literature.* Trans. R. F. C. Hull. Vol. XV of *The Collected Works of C. G. Jung.* Bollingen Series XX. Princeton: Princeton University Press, 1971.

Jung, Emma, and Marie Louise von Franz. *The Grail Legend.* Trans. Andrea Dykes. New York: G. P. Putnam's Sons for the C. G. Jung Foundation for Analytical Psychology, 1970.

Kaplan, Sydney. "An Introduction to *Pym.*" *Poe: A Collection of Critical Essays.* Ed. Robert Regan. Englewood Cliffs, N. J.: Prentice-Hall, 1967, pp. 145-63.

Keats, John. *The Letters of John Keats.* Ed. Maurice Buxton Forman. 2nd ed. New York: Oxford University Press, 1935.

———. *Poetical Works.* Ed. Heathcote William Garrod. Oxford: Clarendon Press, 1958; first ed. 1939.

Keats, John. *The Letters of John Keats: 1814-1821.* Ed. Hyder Edward Rollins. 2 vols. Cambridge, Mass.: Harvard University Press, 1958.

Kendall, Lyle H. "The Vampire Motif in 'The Fall of the House of Usher,' " *College English,* 34 (1963), 450-53.

Krutch, Joseph Wood. *Edgar Allan Poe; A Study in Genius.* New York: A. A. Knopf, 1926.

LaGuardia, David M. "Poe, *Pym* and Initiation." *Emerson Society Quarterly,* No. 60 (1970), pp. 82-84.

Laing, R. D. *The Divided Self: An Existential Study in Sanity and Madness.* New York: Penguin, 1970.

Lastra, Pedro, and Graciela Coulson. "El motivo del horror en *Octaedro.*" *Nueva narrativa hispanoamericana,* 5 (Jan.-Sept. 1975), 7-16.

Lawrence, David Herbert. "Edgar Allan Poe." *Selected Literary Criticism.* Ed. Anthony Beal. New York: Compass-Viking, 1966, pp. 330-46.

Levin, Harry. *The Power of Blackness: Hawthorne, Poe, Melville.* New York: Knopf, 1958.

Lezama Lima, José, et al. *Cinco miradas sobre Cortázar.* Buenos Aires: Tiempo Contemporáneo, 1968.

Lovecraft, Howard Phillips. *Supernatural Horror in Literature.* Introd. E. F. Bleiler. New York: Dover, 1973.

Marcuse, Herbert. *Eros and Civilization: A Philosophical Inquiry into Freud.* New York: Vintage, 1962.

Matas, Julio. "El contexto moral en algunos cuentos de Julio Cortázar." *Revista Iberoamericana,* 39, No. 84-85 (July-Dec. 1973), 593-610.

Monckton-Milnes, Richard (Lord Houghton). *Life and Letters of John Keats.* 1848; rpt. London: J. M. Dent & Sons, 1969.

Murry, John Middleton. *Keats and Shakespeare: A Study of Keats's Poetic Life from 1816 to 1820.* London: Oxford University Press, 1926.

———. *Keats.* New York: Minerva Press, 1968; first ed. entitled *Studies in Keats,* 1930; second ed. entitled *Studies in Keats: New and Old,* 1939; third ed. entitled *The Mystery of Keats,* 1949.

Neumann, Erich. *The Origins and History of Consciousness.* Trans. R. F. C. Hull. Foreword by C. G. Jung. Bollingen Series XLII. Princeton: Princeton University Press, 1971; first ed. in German, 1949.

———. *The Great Mother: An Analysis of the Archetype.* Trans. Ralph Manheim. Bollingen Series XLVII. 2nd ed. Princeton: Princeton University Press, 1972; first ed. 1955.

Neumann, Erich. *Art and the Creative Unconscious*. Trans. Ralph Manheim. Bollingen Series LXI. 2nd ed. Princeton: Princeton University Press, 1972; first ed. 1959.

Perry, Marvin B., Jr. "Keats and Poe." *English Studies in Honor of James Southall Wilson*. Charlottesville: University of Virginia Press, 1951, pp. 45-52.

Picon-Garfield, Evelyn. "Cortázar a continuación . . . con una diferencia." Paper read at the Julio Cortázar Symposium, University of Oklahoma (Norman), November 21-22, 1975.

——. *¿Es Julio Cortázar un surrealista?* Madrid: Gredos, 1975.

Pizarnik, Alejandra. "Nota sobre un cuento de Cortázar: 'El otro cielo.' " *La vuelta a Cortázar en nueve ensayos*. Ed. Néstor Tirri. Buenos Aires: Carlos Pérez, 1967.

Plochmann, George Kimball. *Plato: A Comprehensive Analysis and Selections from His Works*. New York: Dell, 1973.

Poe, Edgar Allan. *The Works of Edgar Allan Poe*. Ed. John H. Ingram. Standard ed. 4 vols. New York: A. C. Armstrong & Son, 1884.

——. *The Complete Works of Edgar Allan Poe*. Ed. James A. Harrison. Virginia ed. 17 vols. New York: T. Y. Crowell, 1902.

——. *Poe's Poems and Essays*. Ed. and introd. by Andrew Lang. London: Everyman, 1927.

Pollin, Burton R. *Dictionary of Names and Titles in Poe's Collected Works*. New York: Da Capo Press, 1968.

Praz, Mario. *The Romantic Agony*. London: Oxford University Press, 1970; first ed. 1930.

Quinn, Arthur Hobson. *Edgar Allan Poe: A Critical Biography*. New York: Appleton, Century, Crofts, 1941.

Quinn, Patrick T. *The French Face of Edgar Poe*. Carbondale: Southern Illinois University Press, 1957.

Rahv, Philip. Introd. to *The Possessed*. By Fyodor M. Dostoievsky. Trans. Constance Garnett. Greenwich, Conn.: Fawcett, 1966.

Rank, Otto. *The Double: A Psychoanalytic Study*. Trans. and ed. with an introd. by Harry Tucker, Jr. Chapel Hill: University of North Carolina Press, 1971; first pub. as *Der Doppelgänger*, 1925.

Regan, Robert, ed. *Poe: A Collection of Critical Essays*. Englewood Cliffs, N. J.: Prentice-Hall, 1967.

Rein, Mercedes. *Cortázar y Carpentier*. Montevideo: Ediciones de Crisis, 1974.

Richardson, Joanna. *Fanny Brawne: A Biography.* London: Thames & Hudson, 1952.

Rimbaud, Arthur. *Poésies complètes.* Ed. Pascal Pia. Paris: Le Livre de Poche, 1963.

Rivera, Ignasi, ed. *Literatura y arte nuevo en Cuba.* Barcelona: Editorial Estela, 1971.

Rivera, Jorge B. "Lo arquetípico en la narrativa argentina del 40." *Nueva novela latino-americana.* Comp. J. Lafforgue. II. Buenos Aires: Paidós, 1974, 174-264.

Rodríguez-Monegal, Emir. "Le Fantôme de Lautréamont." *Review,* Winter 1972, pp. 26-31.

Róheim, Géza. *Magic and Schizophrenia.* Ed. Warner Müensterberger and S. H. Posinsky. Bloomington: Indiana University Press, 1962; first pub. 1955.

Ronay, Gabriel. *The Truth About Dracula.* New York: Stein and Day, 1973; first pub. as *The Dracula Myth,* 1972.

Roy, Joaquín. *Julio Cortázar ante su sociedad.* Barcelona: Península, 1974.

Runciman, Steven. *Byzantine Civilization.* New York: Meridian, 1956.

Salinas, Pedro. "Poe in Spain and Spanish America." In *Poe in Foreign Lands and Tongues: A Symposium.* Baltimore: University of Maryland Press, 1941.

Seylaz, Louis. *Edgar Poe et les premiers symbolistes français.* Lausanne: Plon, 1923.

Sherwood, Margaret. "Keats's Imaginative Approach to Myth." *Undercurrents of Influence in English Romantic Poetry.* Cambridge, Mass.: Harvard University Press, 1934, pp. 203-64.

Silberer, Herbert. *Hidden Symbolism of Alchemy and the Occult Arts.* Trans. Smith Ely Jeliffe. Orig. pub. as *Problems of Mysticism and Its Symbolism,* 1917; rpt. New York: Dover, 1971.

Sola, Graciela de. *Proyecciones del surrealismo en la literatura argentina.* Buenos Aires: Ediciones Culturales Argentinas, 1967.

———. *Julio Cortázar y el hombre nuevo.* Buenos Aires: Sudamericana, 1968.

Sosnowski, Saúl. "Los ensayos de Julio Cortázar: pasos hacia su poética." *Revista Ibero-americana,* 39, No. 84-85 (July-Dec. 1973), 657-66.

———. *Julio Cortázar: una búsqueda mítica.* Buenos Aires: Noé, 1974.

Steinbrunner, Chris, and Burt Goldblatt. *Cinema of the Fantastic.* New York: Gallahad Books, 1972.

Stovall, Floyd, ed. *Eight American Authors: A Review of Research and Criticism.* New York: Modern Language Association of America, 1956.

Stovall, Floyd. "*The Narrative of Arthur Gordon Pym* by Edgar Allan Poe, with an introduction by Richard Wilbur. (Boston: David R. Godine, 1973)." In *The Poe Messenger*, 5, No. 1 (Fall 1974), 6.

Stroupe, John H. "Poe's Imaginary Voyage: Pym as Hero." *Studies in Short Fiction*, 4 (1967), 315-21.

Summers, Montague. *The Vampyre in Europe*. New York: University Books, 1968.

Tate, Allan. "A Reading of Keats." *The American Scholar*, 15 (Winter-Spring 1945-46), 55-63.

———. "The Angelic Imagination." *The Recognition of Edgar Allan Poe*. Ed. Eric W. Carlson. Ann Arbor: University of Michigan, 1966, pp. 236-54.

———. "Our Cousin, Mr. Poe." *Poe: A Collection of Critical Essays*. Ed. Robert Regan. Englewood Cliffs, N. J.: Prentice-Hall, 1967, pp. 38-50.

Thompson, G. R. "Unity, Death, and Nothingness: Poe's 'Romantic Skepticism.' " *PMLA*, 85 (1970), 297-300.

———. *Poe's Fiction*. Madison: University of Wisconsin Press, 1973.

Thorpe, Clarence De Witt. *The Mind of John Keats*. New York: Oxford University Press, 1926.

Tirri, Néstor. "El perseguidor perseguido." *La vuelta a Cortázar en nueve ensayos*. Ed. Néstor Tirri. Buenos Aires: Carlos Pérez, 1968.

Todorov, Tzvetan. *Introduction à la littérature fantastique*. Paris: Seuil (Poétique), 1970.

Van Ghent, Dorothy. "Keats's Myth of the Hero." *Keats-Shelley Journal*, 3 (1954), 7-25.

Ward, Aileen. *John Keats: The Making of a Poet*. New York: Compass-Viking, 1967.

Wilbur, Richard. "The House of Poe." *Poe: A Collection of Critical Essays*. Ed. Robert Regan. Englewood Cliffs, N. J.: Prentice-Hall, 1967.

Yurkievich, Saúl. "Julio Cortázar: al unísono y al dísono." *Revista Iberoamericana*, 39, No. 84-85 (July-Dec. 1973), 411-24.

In the PURDUE UNIVERSITY MONOGRAPHS IN ROMANCE LANGUAGES series the following monographs have been published thus far:

1. *John R. Beverley:* Aspects of Gongóra's 'Soledades'.
   Amsterdam, 1980. iv, 139 pp. Bound.

2. *Robert Francis Cook:* 'Chanson d'Antioche', chanson de geste: Le cycle de la croisade est il épique?
   Amsterdam, 1980. vi, 107 pp. Bound.

3. *Sandy Petrey:* History in the Text: 'Quatrevingt-Treize' and the French Revolution.
   Amsterdam, 1980. viii, 129 pp. Bound.

4. *Walter Kasell:* Marcel Proust and the Strategy of Reading.
   Amsterdam, 1980. x, 125 pp. Bound.

5. *Inéz Azar:* Discurso retórico y mundo pastoral en la 'Egloga segunda' de Garcilaso.
   Amsterdam, 1981. x, 172 pp. Bound.

6. *Roy Armes:* The Films of Alain Robbe-Grillet.
   Amsterdam, 1981. x, 217 pp. Bound.

7. *Le 'Galien' de Cheltenham,* édité par David M. Dougherty & Eugène B. Barnes.
   Amsterdam, 1981. xxxvii, 203 pp. Bound.

8. *Ana Hernández del Castillo:* Keats, Poe, and the Shaping of Cortázar's Mythopoesis.
   Amsterdam, 1981. xii, 135 pp. Bound.

9. *Carlos Albarracín-Sarmiento:* Estructura del 'Martín Fierro'.
   Amsterdam, 1981. xx, 336 pp. Bound.